*This handbook is dedicated t... and
supports and to all who love and support them.*

**The implementation of the new federal rules governing the
operation of nursing homes in the United States covers a
multi-year time span. The first and largest set became
effective November 28, 2016. On November 28, 2017,
additional rules were implemented along with a complete
revision of the codes associated with them, known as F-Tags. A
much smaller additional set of new regulations will be
implemented in Phase III.**

*At least 60% of any profits from this handbook will be donated to Voices
for Quality Care.*

<u>NOTICE</u>

The Center for Medicare and Medicaid Services (CMS) has declared a temporary 18-month moratorium on the full enforcement of a few of the Phase II regulations that became effective on November 28, 2017. The moratorium affects the imposition of civil money penalties (CMPs), discretionary denials of payment for new admissions (DPNAs) and discretionary termination. Those regulations affect only a few of the Phase II regulations associated with F-Tags included in this manual. They are

- F655 (Baseline Care Plan);
- F740 (Behavioral Health Services);
- F741 (Sufficient/Competent Direct Care/Access Staff-Behavioral Health);
- F758 (Psychotropic Medications) related to PRN Limitations;
- F926 (Smoking Policies).

We have included notations on this moratorium in the FOR VOICES FOR QUALITY CARE ADVOCATES Section of these F-Tags.

Table of Contents

6

NOTES

Acronyms

AAA (Triple A)—Area Agency on Aging

ACL—Administration for Community Living
AARP—American Association of Retired Persons
ABI—Acquired Brain Injury
AC—Before a meal
ACA—Affordable Care Act
ADA—Americans with Disabilities Act
ADC—Adult Day Care
ADL—Activities of Daily Living
ADR—Adverse Drug Reaction
ADRC—Aging, Disabled Resource Center (Maryland)
AES—Adaptive Equipment Specialist
AG—Attorney General
AHCA—American Health Care Association
AHLA—American Health Lawyers Association
ALF—Assisted Living Facility
ANSI—American National Standards Institute
AOA—Administration on Aging (Federal)
APS—Adult Protective Services
ASPE—Assistant Secretary for Planning and Evaluation (DHHS)
AT—Assistive Technology

BCBA— Board Certified Behavior Analyst
BD—Twice a day / Bipolar Disorder
BGL—Blood Glucose Level
BP—Blood Pressure
BPSD—Behavioral or Psychological Symptoms of Dementia

CAH—Care At Home
CAP—Client Assistance Program
CARE—Consumer/Advocate Review & Eval.
CARF—Com. on Accreditation of Rehab. Facilities
CASPER—Certification and Survey Provider Enhanced Reports
CBO—Community Based Organization

CDC—Centers for Disease Control & Prevention
CEO—Chief Executive Officer
CHHA—Certified Home Health Agency
CHIP—Children's Health Insurance Program
CIL—Centers for Independent Living
CIN—Client Identification Number (Medicaid)
CLIA—Clinical Laboratory Improvement Amendment
CMCM—Comprehensive Medicaid Case Management
CMS—Center for Medicare & Medicaid Services
CNS—Clinical Nurse Specialist
CON—Certificate of Need
COPD—Chronic Obstructive Pulmonary Disease
CP—Cerebral Palsy
CPR—Cardiopulmonary Resuscitation

DA—Developmental Aide
DC—Developmental Center
DD—Developmental Disabilities
DHS—Department of Human Services (MD)
DHMH—Department of Health & Mental Hygiene (MD)
DME—Durable Medical Equipment
DNR—Do Not Resuscitate
DOB—Date of Birth
DOH—Department of Health (DC)
DoN—Director of Nursing
DVA—Division of Veterans Affairs

EBT—Electronic Benefit Transfer
EEOC—Equal Employment Opportunity Commission
EHB—Essential Health Benefits
EHR—Electronic Health Record
EI—Early Intervention
EO—Executive Order
ESL—English as a Second Language

FDA—Food and Drug Administration (Federal)
FOIA—Freedom of Information Act (Federal)
FTE—Full Time Equivalent

FY—Fiscal Year

GA—Geriatric Aide
GAAP—Generally Accepted Accounting Principles
GAO—Government Accountability Office (US)
GED—General Education Diploma

HACCP—Hazard Analysis and Critical Control Point
HAI—Healthcare-Associated Infection
HCBSW—Home & Community Based Settings
HHS—U.S. Dept. of Health & Human Services
HIPAA—Health Insurance Portability & Accountability Act
HIV—Human Immunodeficiency Virus (AIDS)
HMO—Health Management Organization
HUD—Housing & Urban Development

ICN—International Council of Nurses
IDT—Interdisciplinary Team
IDEA—Individuals with Disabilities Education Act
IESNA—Illuminating Engineering Society of North America
IG—Interpretive Guidance
ILC—Independent Living Center
IP—Infection Preventionist
IPCP—Infection Prevention and Control Program
IT—Interdisciplinary Team
IT—Information Technology

JCAH—Joint Commission on the Accreditation of Hospitals

LCED—Level of Care Eligibility Determination
LCSW—Licensed Clinical Social Worker

LGU—Local Government Unit
LHA—Local Housing Authorities
LHCSA—Licensed Home Care Services Agency
LLTCOP—Local Long Term Care Ombudsman Program
LOC—Level of Care
LPN—Licensed Practical Nurse

LRE—Least Restrictive Environment
LSC—Life Safety Code
LSW—Licensed Social Worker
LTC—Long-Term Care
LTCOP—Long Term Care Ombudsman Program
LTSS—Long Term Services and Supports

MA—Medicaid
MAR—Medication Administration Record
MCO—Managed Care Organization
MDS—Minimum Data Set
MDLC—Maryland Disabilities Law Center
MDOA—Maryland Department of Aging
MFP—Money Follows the Person
MH—Mental Health
MMIS—Medicaid Management Information System
MOU—Memorandum of Understanding
MPIA—Maryland Public Information Act

NA—Nurse Aide
NATCEP—Nurse Aide Training Competency Evaluation Program
NF—Nursing Facility
NIA—National Institute on Aging
NIH—National Institutes of Health
NIMBY—Not In My Back Yard
NIMH—National Institute of Mental Health
NP—Nurse Practitioner

OAA—Older Americans Act
OCFS—Office of Children & Family Services
OIG—Office of the Inspector General
OMB—Office of Management and Budget
ONC—Office of the National Coordinator
OSHA—Occupational Safety & Health Administration
OT—Occupational Therapy
OTR—Registered Occupational Therapist

PA—Physician's Assistant

PA—Public Assistance
PASARR—Preadmission Screening & Annual Resident Review
PCP—Person Centered Planning
PEU—Protein-Energy under Nutrition
PIA—Patient Income Account
PIA—Personal Incidental Allowance
PIPs—Performance Improvement Projects
POCA—Plan of Corrective Action
PRI—Patient Review Instrument
PRN—As needed
PS—Personal Service
PT—Physical Therapy
PWS—Prader Willi Syndrome

QA—Quality Assurance
QAA—Quality Assessment and Assurance
QAPI—Quality Assurance Performance Improvement
QI—Quality Indicator
QI/QM—Quality Indicator/Quality Measure
QIO—Quality Improvement Organization

RFA—Regulatory Flexibility Act
RN—Registered Nurse
RSVP—Retired Senior Volunteer Program

SD—Self Determination
SLP—Speech/Language Pathology
SNF—Skilled Nursing Facility
SOD—Statement of Deficiency
SP—Speech Pathology
SRU—Small Residential Unit
SSA—Social Security Administration
SSDI—Social Security Disability Insurance
SSI—Supplemental Security Income

TA—Temporary Assistance
TBI—Traumatic Brain Injury
TF—Transitional Funding

TRO—Temporary Restraining Order
TTY—Text Telephone (for hearing impaired)
TUBS—Temporary Use Beds

UCPA—United Cerebral Palsy Association
UTI—Urinary Tract Infection

VA—Veterans Administration

WHO- World Health Organization

HIPAA

FOR VOICES FOR QUALITY CARE ADVOCATES

We've heard nursing home staff refuse to allow people living in the home to discuss their personal care issues with anyone, including in Resident Council meetings, by claiming HIPAA forbids it.

Individuals have the right not only to view their own records but also to show them to anyone they choose and to talk about them in any setting they choose. The same applies to anyone who is a Health Surrogate, who holds a Power of Attorney, or is a Guardian for a person living in a nursing home, an assisted living facility, a hospital, or in any other health care setting.

We've encountered numerous instances where staff insists that HIPAA allows only the resident or the resident's representative to view the records. This also is untrue. The resident or the resident's legal representative can show the records to anyone they choose. They can publish them in the local paper if they choose although we most certainly wouldn't recommend it. They do not need to fill out or sign any forms to do this.

We have encountered this use of HIPAA to prevent the legitimate sharing of medical records a number of times when staff inaccurately tries to insist that Voices volunteers cannot review records with a client, using HIPAA as the excuse.

DEFINING THE LAW

HIPAA (Health Insurance Portability and Accountability Act of 1996) is a federal law and applies to the entire country. It contains a privacy act that forbids medical personnel from sharing health information without express permission of the person involved. It is also one of the most misunderstood laws governing long term care situations.

This law and its regulations <u>apply</u> to all "covered entities".
These "covered entities" include:

- Health Plans
  - Health Plans: insurance companies
  - HMO's
  - Company health plans
  - Certain government programs that pay for health care
    - including Medicare and Medicaid
- Most Health Care Providers
  - Electronic billing services
  - Most doctors
  - Clinics
  - Hospitals
  - Psychologists
  - Chiropractors
  - Nursing homes
  - Pharmacies
  - Dentists
- Health Care Clearinghouses
- Business Associates of Covered Entities
  - Physician billing companies
  - Companies processing health care claims
  - Companies that help administer health plans
  - Outside lawyers, accountants, and IT specialists
  - Companies that store or destroy records

This law and its regulations <u>do not apply</u> to the following organizations or persons.

- *The person for whom the records are written (and their legal representatives)*
  - Life insurers

- o Employers
- o Workers compensation carriers
- o Most schools and school districts
- o Many state agencies
  - Child protective service agencies
  - Adult protective services agencies
- Most law enforcement agencies
- Many municipal offices

The information above was taken primarily from the HHS website. For more information on HIPAA or for information in other languages, go to the HHS website: http://www.hhs.gov/ocr/privacy/hipaa/understanding/index.html

This law protects information about you that your doctors, nurses, and other health care providers put into your medical records, conversations about your care or treatment with those persons, information about you in your insurer's computer system, billing information, and most other health information.

It does not cover anyone that the persons about whom the records are written or their representatives allow to view these records including

- Family
- Friends
- Relatives
- Advocates
- Media Representatives
- Or anyone else

Federal Nursing Home Regulations

The regulations in this handbook are those that became effective on November 28, 2017. These regulations are important because they are the basis for the rights everyone living in a nursing home and their representatives and family members should enjoy.

Regulations that are not often used by Voices Advocates have been omitted. For those and for additional information on all of the regulations, see the Surveyor's Guidelines using the URL below. The Surveyor's Guidelines are the federal "rules" that are used by state nursing home Surveyors and Complaint Investigators to identify and cite nursing homes that are in violation of these regulations.

URL for the <u>draft</u> of the new Surveyor's Guidelines quoted in this addendum.

https://www.cms.gov/Medicare/Provider-Enrollment-and-Certification/GuidanceforLawsAndRegulations/Downloads/Advance-Appendix-PP-Including-Phase-2-.pdf

Although federal nursing home regulations—and some state regulations—have been in effect for 28 years, many people working in nursing homes and most people living in nursing homes and their friends and families are not fully familiar with these regulations. Often, staff members have good intentions but trample on residents' rights in a misguided attempt to "protect" those under their care. Examples are staff attempts to curtail visits by family members or to deny access to medical records.

As a part of Voices mission to foster compliance with long term care regulations, we have published our Handbook and this Supplement as a reference source. In this publication we have included the new regulations and the new F-tag numbers associated with them. F-Tags (F540, etc.) are the coding system used to identify the different regulations. Where appropriate, we have also included specific Maryland and Washington DC laws and regulations relating to specific federal regulations.

For additional sources of information see the list of helpful URLs at the end of this publication.

In this section,

Current regulatory language is presented in normal font.

New regulatory language is present in **bold italics**.

New regulatory language that would normally be presented in bold font as a part of a section code or title is presented in **<u>underlined, italicized bold.</u>**

F540—Definitions

NOTE: Additional definitions can be found under the various F-Tags.

Abuse.

Abuse is the willful infliction of injury, unreasonable confinement, intimidation, or punishment with resulting physical harm, pain or mental anguish. Abuse also includes the deprivation by an individual, including a caretaker, of goods or services that are necessary to attain or maintain physical, mental, and psychosocial well-being. Instances of abuse of all residents, irrespective of any mental or physical condition, cause physical harm, pain or mental anguish. It includes verbal abuse, sexual abuse, physical abuse, and mental abuse including abuse facilitated or enabled through the use of technology. Willful, as used in this definition of abuse, means the individual must have acted deliberately, not that the individual must have intended to inflict injury or harm.

Adverse event.

An adverse event is an untoward, undesirable, and usually unanticipated event that causes death or serious injury, or the risk thereof.

Common area.

Common areas are areas in the facility where residents may gather together with other residents, visitors, and staff *or engage in individual pursuits, apart from their residential rooms. This includes but is not limited to living rooms, dining rooms,* activity rooms, *outdoor areas*, and meeting rooms where residents are located on a regular basis.

Composite distinct part.

Definition. A composite distinct part is a distinct part consisting of two or more non- contiguous components that are not located within the same campus, as defined in §413.65(a)(2) of this chapter.

> **Maryland does not really have distinct parts in nursing homes since facilities accepting Medicaid and/or Medicare**

have all beds certified for Medicaid and/or Medicare. For a more detailed definition see the Surveyor's Guidelines.

Distinct part

Definition. A distinct part SNF or NF is physically distinguishable from the larger institution or institutional complex that houses it, meets the requirements of this paragraph and of paragraph (2) of this definition, and meets the applicable statutory requirements for SNFs or NFs in sections 1819 or 1919 of the Act, respectively.

Maryland does not really have distinct parts in nursing homes since facilities accepting Medicaid and/or Medicare have all beds certified for Medicaid and/or Medicare. For a more detailed definition see the Surveyor's Guidelines.

Exploitation.

Exploitation means taking advantage of a resident for personal gain through the use of manipulation, intimidation, threats, or coercion.

Facility defined.

For this definition see the Surveyor's Guidelines.

Fully sprinklered.

A fully sprinklered long term care facility is one that has all areas sprinklered in accordance with National Fire Protection Association 13 "Standard for the Installation of Sprinkler Systems" without the use of waivers or the Fire Safety Evaluation System

Licensed health professional.

A licensed health professional is a physician; physician assistant; nurse practitioner; physical, speech, or occupational therapist; physical or occupational therapy assistant; registered professional nurse; licensed practical nurse; or licensed or certified social worker; or registered respiratory therapist or certified respiratory therapy technician.

Major modification

Major Modification means the modification of more than 50 percent, or more than 4,500 square feet, of the smoke compartment

Misappropriation of resident property

Misappropriation of resident property means the deliberate misplacement, exploitation, or wrongful, temporary, or permanent use of a resident's belongings or money without the resident's consent.

Mistreatment

Mistreatment means inappropriate treatment or exploitation of a resident.

Neglect

Neglect is the failure of the facility, its employees or service providers to provide goods and services to a resident that are necessary to avoid physical harm, pain, mental anguish, or emotional distress.

Nurse aide.

A nurse aide is any individual providing nursing or nursing-related services to residents in a facility. This term may also include an individual who provides these services through an agency or under a contract with the facility, but is not a licensed health professional, a registered dietitian, or someone who volunteers to provide such services without pay. Nurse aides do not include those individuals who furnish services to residents only as paid feeding assistants as defined in §488.301 of this chapter.

Person-centered care.

For purposes of this subpart, person-centered care means to focus on the resident as the locus of control and support the resident in making their own choices and having control over their daily lives.

Resident representative.

For purposes of this subpart, the term resident representative means any of the following:

(1) An individual chosen by the resident to act on behalf of the resident in order to support the resident in decision-making; access medical,

social or other personal information of the resident; manage financial matters; or receive notifications;

(2) A person authorized by State or Federal law (including but not limited to agents under power of attorney, representative payees, and other fiduciaries) to act on behalf of the resident in order to support the resident in decision-making; access medical, social or other personal information of the resident; manage financial matters; or receive notifications; or

(3) Legal representative, as used in section 712 of the Older Americans Act; or

(4) The court-appointed guardian or conservator of a resident.

(5) Nothing in this rule is intended to expand the scope of authority of any resident representative beyond that authority specifically authorized by the resident, State or Federal law, or a court of competent jurisdiction.

Sexual abuse

Sexual abuse is non-consensual sexual contact of any type with a resident.

Transfer and discharge

Sexual abuse is non-consensual sexual contact of any type with a resident.

Transfer and discharge

Transfer and discharge includes movement of a resident to a bed outside of the certified facility whether that bed is in the same physical plant or not. Transfer and discharge does not refer to movement of a resident to a bed within the same certified facility.

#

483.10 Resident Rights

This section contains F-Tags 550-586 which cover the regulations in §483.10

F550—Resident Rights/Exercise of Rights

FOR VOICES FOR QUALITY CARE ADVOCATES

Civil Rights: People living in long term care facilities retain all of the rights of US citizens including the right to be informed voters. This means the right to communicate with legislators and persons running for office as well as the right to vote. Be aware of practices that infringe on these rights.

For "Justice Involved Residents", people living in nursing homes who are in legal custody, under legal supervision, or in similar legal positions see the Surveyor's Guidelines for rights directly applicable to these individuals.

THE REGULATIONS

§483.10(a) Resident Rights.

The resident has a right to a dignified existence, self-determination, and communication with and access to persons and services inside and outside the facility, *including those specified in this section.*

§483.10(a)(1) A facility must *treat each resident with respect and dignity and care for each resident* in a manner and in an environment that promotes maintenance or enhancement *of his or her* quality of life, *recognizing each resident's individuality. The facility must protect and promote the rights of the resident.*

§483.10(a)(2) The facility must provide equal access to quality care regardless of diagnosis, severity of condition, or payment source. A facility must establish and maintain identical policies and practices regarding transfer, discharge,

and the provision of services under the State plan for all residents regardless of payment source.

§483.10(b) **Exercise of Rights**. The resident has the right to exercise his or her rights as a resident of the facility and as a citizen or resident of the United States.

§483.10(b)(1) The facility must ensure that the resident can exercise his or her rights without interference, coercion, discrimination, or reprisal from the facility.

*§483.10(b)(*2) The resident has the right to be free of interference, coercion, discrimination, and reprisal from the facility in exercising his or her rights *and to be supported by the facility in the exercise of his or her rights as required under this subpart.*

GUIDANCE: FROM THE SURVEYOR'S GUIDELINES

Examples of treating residents with dignity and respect include, but are not limited to:

- Encouraging and assisting residents to dress in their own clothes, *rather than hospital- type gowns, and appropriate footwear for* the time of day and individual preferences;

- *Placing labels* on each resident's clothing in a way that *is inconspicuous and* respects his or her dignity (*for example*, placing labeling on the inside of shoes and clothing *or using a color coding system);*

- Promoting resident independence and dignity while dining, such as avoiding:

  o Daily use of disposable cutlery and dishware;

  o Bibs or clothing protectors instead of napkins (except by resident choice);

- o Staff standing over residents while assisting them to eat;

- o Staff interacting/conversing only with each other rather than with residents while assisting with meals;

- ***Protecting and valuing residents'*** private space (***for example***, knocking on doors and requesting permission before entering, closing doors as requested by the resident*);*

- ***Staff should*** address residents with ***the*** name ***or pronoun*** of the resident's choice, avoid***ing the*** use of labels for residents such as "feeders" ***or "walkers." Residents should*** not ***be*** exclud***ed*** from conversations ***during activities or when care is being provided, nor should staff*** discuss residents ***in settings where*** others can overhear private or protected information ***or document in charts/electronic health records where others can see a resident's information;***

- Refraining from practices demeaning to residents such as ***leaving*** urinary catheter bags uncovered, refusing to comply with a resident's request for ***bathroom*** assistance during meal times, and restricting residents from use of common areas open to the general public such as lobbies and restrooms, unless they are on transmission-based isolation precautions or are restricted according to their care planned needs.

F551—Rights Exercised by Representative

FOR VOICES FOR QUALITY CARE ADVOCATES

We continually receive requests for assistance in cases where Resident Representative rights are challenged by facility staff.

- Nursing home staff tries to convince vulnerable person to override the decisions of the POA.
- Resident Representatives are not immediately consulted before transfers to hospital, before medications are changed, before new medical orders are implemented, and when the resident's condition changes.

Power of Attorney or Guardianship: Where these exist, the facility should have documentation and that should be available in the Resident's records.

- Resident Representatives — Don't just "visit", participate.
- Review records with particular attention to the medicine list, daily treatment chart, care plan, and (in Maryland) MOLST form.
- Join the Family Council.
- Be aware of your rights and the rights of the Resident. Advocates fought hard for these rights. Use them!

Assisted Living Facilities and other Long Term Care Settings:

People living in assisted living or other long term care situations do not have these carefully articulated rights. But, they do have all of the protections of people living elsewhere in the community.

THE REGULATIONS

§483.10(b)(3) In the case of a resident who has not been adjudged incompetent *by the state court, the resident has the right to designate a representative,* in accordance with State law and any legal surrogate *so* designated may exercise the resident's rights to the extent provided by state law. *The same-sex spouse of a resident must be afforded treatment equal to that afforded to an opposite-sex spouse if the marriage was valid in the jurisdiction in which it was celebrated*

- *(1) The resident representative has the right to exercise the resident's rights to the extent those rights are delegated to the representative.*
- *(2) The resident retains the right to exercise those rights not delegated to a resident representative, including the right to revoke a delegation of rights, except as limited by State law.*
- *§483.10(b)(4) The facility must treat the decisions of a resident representative as the decisions of the resident to the extent required by the court or delegated by the resident, in accordance with applicable law.*
- *§483.10(b)(5) The facility shall not extend the resident representative the right to make decisions on behalf of the resident beyond the extent required by the court or delegated by the resident, in accordance with applicable law.*
- *§483.10(b)(6) If the facility has reason to believe that a resident representative is making decisions or taking actions that are not in the best interests of a resident, the facility shall report such concerns when and in the manner required under State law.*
- *§483.10(b)(7)* In the case of a resident adjudged incompetent under the laws of a State by a court of competent jurisdiction, the rights of the resident *devolve to and* are exercised by *the resident representative* appointed under State law to act on the resident's behalf. *The court- appointed resident representative exercises the resident's rights to the extent judged necessary by a court of competent jurisdiction, in accordance with State law.*
  - *(i) In the case of a resident representative whose decision-making authority is limited by State law or*

court appointment, the resident retains the right to make those decisions outside the representative's authority.

- o *(ii) The resident's wishes and preferences must be considered in the exercise of rights by the representative.*
- o *(iii) To the extent practicable, the resident must be provided with opportunities to participate in the care planning process.*
- o

DEFINITIONS

"Court of competent jurisdiction"

means any court with the authority to hear and determine a case or suit with the matter in question.

"Resident representative"

For purposes of this subpart, the term resident representative may mean any of the following:

1. An individual chosen by the resident to act on behalf of the resident in order to support the resident in decision-making; access medical, social or other personal information of the resident; manage financial matters; or receive notifications;

2. A person authorized by State or Federal law (including but not limited to agents under power of attorney, representative payees, and other fiduciaries) to act on behalf of the resident in order to support the resident in decision-making; access medical, social or other personal information of the resident; manage financial matters; or receive notifications; or

3. Legal representative, as used in section 712 of the Older Americans Act; or

4. The court-appointed guardian or conservator of a resident.

5. Nothing in this rule is intended to expand the scope of authority of any resident representative beyond that authority specifically authorized by the resident, State or Federal law, or a court of competent jurisdiction

GUIDANCE: EXERPTS FROM THE SURVEYOR'S GUIDELINES

KEY ELEMENTS OF NONCOMPLIANCE §§483.10(b)(3)-(7)

To cite deficient practice at F551, the surveyor's investigation will generally show that the facility failed to do any one or more of the following:

- *Ensure a competent resident's choice for a representative is honored or*
- *Ensure that treatment of a same-sex spouse was the same as treatment of an opposite-sex spouse; or*
- *Ensure the resident representative did not make decisions beyond the extent allowed by the court or delegated by the resident; or*
- *Ensure the resident's wishes and preferences were considered when decisions were made by the resident representative; or*
- *Ensure the decisions of the resident representative are given the same consideration as if the resident made the decision themselves; or*
- *Honor the resident's authority to exercise his or her rights, even when he or she has delegated those rights, including the right to revoke a delegation of rights; or*
- *Ensure the resident representative was reported as State law required when not acting in the best interest of the resident; or*
- *Ensure a resident who was found incompetent by the court is provided with opportunities to participate in the care planning process.*

F552—Right to be Informed/Make Treatment Decisions

FOR VOICES FOR QUALITY CARE ADVOCATES

CAUTION: be alert to violations of this regulation

The current regulation has been modified to make it clearer that the resident or the resident's representative **must** be notified **and must give consent** to any change in care **before** it is initiated. This includes any changes in medications.

In a language you understand means your native tongue or a language in which you are fully comfortable conversing and exchanging ideas. This may mean using an interpreter at no cost to you.

For persons with hearing impairments, this means oral, cued, signed English, or American Sign Language interpreters. These interpreters must be available whenever questions of any kind arise.

THE REGULATIONS

§483.10(c) Planning and Implementing Care.

The resident has the right to be informed of, and participate in, his or her treatment, *including:*

§483.10(c)(1) The right to be fully informed in language that he or she can understand of his or her total health status, including but not limited to, his or her medical condition.

§483.10(c)(4) The right to be informed, in advance, *of the* care *to be furnished and the type of care giver or professional that will furnish care.*

§483.10(c)(5) The right to be informed in advance, by the physician or other practitioner or professional, of the risks and benefits of proposed care, of treatment and treatment alternatives or treatment options and to choose the alternative or option he or she prefers.

DEFINITIONS §483.10(c)(1), (4)-(5)

"Total health status"

includes functional status, nutritional status, rehabilitation and restorative potential, ability to participate in activities, cognitive status, oral health status, psychosocial status, and sensory and physical impairments.

"Treatment"

refers to medical care, nursing care, and interventions provided to maintain or restore health and well-being, improve functional level, or relieve symptoms.

GUIDANCE: EXERPTS FROM THE SURVEYOR'S GUIDELINES

Health information **and services** must be **provided in way**s that **are easy for** the resident and/or the resident's representative **to** understand. This includes, **but is not limited to, communicating in plain language, explaining technical and medical terminology in a way that makes sense to the resident, offering language assistance services to residents who have limited English proficiency, and providing qualified sign language interpreters or auxiliary aids if hearing is impaired. This does not mean that a facility is required to supply and pay for hearing aids.**

The physician or other practitioner or professional must inform the resident **or their representative in advance of treatment risks and benefits, options, and alternatives....The resident or resident representative has the right to choose the option he or she prefers.**

# # #

F553—Right to Participate in Planning Care

FOR VOICES FOR QUALITY CARE ADVOCATES

CAUTION: We continually encounter instances in which people living in nursing homes are not involved in their care planning conferences. This seems to be particularly prevalent in situations where family members do not attend. Some people living in nursing homes for long periods of time have not been aware that care conferences were being held.

THE REGULATIONS

§483.10(c)(2) The right to participate in *the development and implementation of his or her person-centered plan of care, including but not limited to:*

- *(i) The right to participate in the planning process, including the right to identify individuals or roles to be included in the planning process, the right to request meetings and the right to request revisions to the person-centered plan of care.*
- *(ii) The right to participate in establishing the expected goals and outcomes of care, the type, amount, frequency, and duration of care, and any other factors related to the effectiveness of the plan of care.*
- *(iii)* The right to be informed, in advance, of changes *to the plan of care.*
- *(iv) The right to receive the services and/or items included in the plan of care.*
- *(v) The right to see the care plan, including the right to sign after significant changes to the plan of care.*

§483.10(c)(3) The facility shall inform the resident of the right to participate in his or her treatment and shall support the resident in this right. The planning process must—

- *(i) Facilitate the inclusion of the resident and/or resident representative.*
- *(ii) Include an assessment of the resident's strengths and needs.*
- *(iii) Incorporate the resident's personal and cultural preferences in developing goals of care.*

INTENT §483.10(c)(2)-(3)

To ensure facility staff facilitates the inclusion of the resident or resident representative in all aspects of person-centered care planning and that this planning includes the provision of services to enable the resident to live with dignity and supports the resident's goals, choices, and preferences including, but not limited to, goals related to the their daily routines and goals to potentially return to a community setting.

GUIDANCE: EXERPTS FROM THE SURVEYOR'S GUIDELINES §483.10(c)(2)-(3)

Residents and their representative(s) must be afforded the opportunity to participate in their care planning process and to be included in decisions and changes in care, treatment, and/or interventions..... Facility staff must support and encourage participation in the care planning process. This may include ..... holding care planning meetings at the time of day when a resident is functioning best, providing sufficient notice in advance of the meeting, scheduling these meetings to accommodate a resident's representative (such as conducting the meeting in-person, via a conference call, or video conferencing), and planning enough time for information exchange and decision making.

# # #

F554—Resident Self-Admin Meds-Clinically Appropriate

FOR VOICES FOR QUALITY CARE ADVOCATES

Residents have the right to manage their medications.

In cases of discharge it is imperative that the person be trained at least 2 weeks in advance of the discharge to either manage their medications or to train the person who will be responsible for the medications to administer them correctly.

THE REGULATIONS

§483.10*(c)(7) The right to* self-administer *medications* if the interdisciplinary team, as defined by §483.*21(b)(2)(ii),* has determined that this practice is *clinically appropriate.*

NOTE: For more information on this regulation see the Surveyor's Guidelines.

###

F555—Right to Choose/Be Informed of Attending Physician

FOR VOICES FOR QUALITY CARE ADVOCATES

This is an issue that Voices Volunteers are frequently called upon to advocate for. It is particularly difficult in some counties in Maryland where physicians who will serve people living in nursing homes are few, leaving those people with limited or no choices of physician. This one requires further advocacy on both state and federal levels. Meantime, here are the current regulations.

THE REGULATIONS

§483.10(d) Choice of Attending Physician. The resident has the right to choose **his or her** attending physician.

§483.10(d)(1) The physician must be licensed to practice, and

§483.10(d)(2) If the physician chosen by the resident refuses to or does not meet requirements specified in this part, the facility may seek alternate physician participation as specified in paragraphs (d)(4) and (5) of this section to assure provision of appropriate and adequate care and treatment.

§483.10(d)(3) The facility must **ensure that** each resident **remains informed** of the name, specialty, and way of contacting the physician **and other primary care professionals** responsible for his or her care.

§483.10(d)(4) The facility must inform the resident if the facility determines that the physician chosen by the resident is unable or unwilling to meet requirements specified in this part and the facility seeks alternate physician participation to assure provision of appropriate and adequate care and treatment. The facility must discuss the alternative physician

participation with the resident and honor the resident's preferences, if any, among options.

§483.10(d)(5) If the resident subsequently selects another attending physician who meets the requirements specified in this part, the facility must honor that choice.

DEFINITIONS §§483.10(d)(1)-(5)

"Attending physician"

refers to the primary physician **who** is responsible for managing the resident's medical care. This does not include other physicians whom the resident may see periodically, such as specialists.

#

F557—Respect, Dignity/Right to have Personal Property

THE REGULATIONS

§483.10(e)(3) The right to reside and receive services in the facility with reasonable accommodation of *resident* needs and preferences except when *to do so would endanger* the health or safety of the *resident* or other residents.

INTENT §483.10(e)(2)

All residents' possessions, regardless of their apparent value to others, must be treated with respect.

GUIDANCE: EXERPTS FROM THE SURVEYOR'S GUIDELINES

The right to retain and use personal possessions *promotes a homelike environment and supports each resident in maintaining their independence.*

If residents' rooms have few personal possessions, ask residents, *their* families, *or representative(s), as well as* the local ombudsman if:

- Residents are encouraged to have and to use them; *and*
- *Residents may choose to retain personal possessions.*

###

F558—Reasonable Accommodations of Needs/Preferences

THE REGULATIONS

§483.10(f)(10) Protection of Resident Funds

The resident has *a* right to manage his or her financial affairs. *This includes the right to know, in advance, what charges a facility may impose against a resident's personal funds.*

INTENT §483.10(e)(3)

The accommodation of resident needs and preferences is essential to creating an individualized, home-like environment.

DEFINITIONS §483.10(e)(3)

"Reasonable accommodation of resident needs and preferences"

means the facility's efforts to individualize the resident's physical environment.

GUIDANCE: EXERPTS FROM THE SURVEYOR'S GUIDELINES §483.10(e)(3)

Reasonable accommodation(s) of resident needs and preferences includes, *but is not limited to, individualizing* the physical environment of the resident's bedroom and bathroom, as well as individualizing *common living areas* as much as feasible......

The environment must reflect the unique needs and preferences *of each resident* to the extent reasonable and does not endanger the health or safety of individuals or other residents.

Common areas frequented by residents should accommodate residents' physical limitations….. Resident seating *should have* appropriate seat height, depth, firmness, and with arms that assist residents to independently rise to a standing position. *Functional furniture must be arranged to accommodate residents' needs and preferences.*

<u>*Examples of noncompliance may include, but are not limited to:*</u>

- *Storing a wheelchair or other adapt equipment out of reach of a resident who is otherwise able to use them independently, such as a wheelchair stored across the room for a resident who is able to self-transfer or storing eyeglasses out of reach for a resident.*
- *Having areas of worship inaccessible to residents with mobility limitations.*
- *Not providing a riser on a toilet to maintain independence.*

F559—Choose/Be Notified of Room/Roommate Change

FOR VOICES FOR QUALITY CARE ADVOCATES

Be aware that Maryland regulations require a 30 day notice of change of rooms within a facility. That regulation is quoted at the end of this section.

When advocating against an involuntary discharge or a transfer to a different facility, be sure to ask for a written copy of the notification of discharge or transfer. We often find that facilities try to convince residents to leave a facility by simply telling them they must leave and hoping they will do so without issuing the required written notices.

In any case of an involuntary discharge or transfer, the case should immediately be referred to the Long-Term Care Project of Legal Aid in Maryland and to the Long-Term Care Ombudsman Program attorney in the District of Columbia.

THE REGULATIONS

§483.10(e)(4) The right to share a room with his or her spouse when married residents live in the same facility and both spouses consent to the arrangement.

§483.10(e)(5) The right to share a room with his or her roommate of choice when practicable, when both residents live in the same facility and both residents consent to the arrangement.

§483.10(e)(6) The right to receive **written** notice, **including the reason for the change,** before the resident's room or roommate in the facility is changed.

GUIDANCE: EXERPTS FROM THE SURVEYOR'S GUIDELINES §483.10(e)(4)-(6)

Residents have the right to share a room with whomever they wish, as long as both residents are in agreement. These arrangements could include opposite-sex and same-sex married couples or domestic partners, siblings, or friends.

There are some limitations to these rights. Residents do not have the right to demand that a current roommate is displaced in order to accommodate the couple that wishes to room together. .....

..... The resident should be provided the opportunity to see the new location, meet the new roommate, and ask questions about the move.

A resident receiving a new roommate should *be* given as much *advance* notice *as possible. The resident* should *be* supported *when a* roommate passes away by providing time to adjust before moving another person into the room. The length of time needed to adjust may differ depending upon the resident. Facility *staff* should provide necessary social services for a resident who is grieving over the death of a roommate.

THE MARYLAND REGULATIONS

10.07.09.12.Resident Relocation and Bed Hold.

A. Notification of Resident Relocation Within a Facility.

- (1) Except in emergency situations or when it is documented in the resident's record that a resident's physical, clinical, or psychological well being would be jeopardized, a nursing facility shall notify a resident or, when applicable, the resident's representative or interested family member, if available, in writing at least 30 days before the resident is relocated within a facility or to a different part of a facility, unless the resident or, if the resident is incapacitated, the resident's legally authorized representative, agrees to the relocation and this is documented in the resident's record.

F560—Right to Refuse Certain Transfers

FOR VOICES FOR QUALITY CARE ADVOCATES

This regulation will apply primarily to people living in nursing homes in states other than Maryland. For additional information consult the Surveyor's Guidelines.

THE REGULATIONS

§483.10(e)(7) The right to refuse to transfer to another room in the facility, if the purpose of the transfer is:

- (i) *to relocate* a resident of a SNF from the distinct part of the institution that is a SNF to a part of the institution that is not a SNF, or
- (ii) *to relocate* a resident of a NF from the distinct part of the institution that is a NF to a distinct part of the institution that is a SNF.
- (iii) *solely for the convenience of staff.*

§483.10(e)(8) A resident's exercise of the right to refuse transfer does not affect the resident's eligibility or entitlement to Medicare or Medicaid benefits.

#

F561—Self Determination

THE REGULATIONS

§483.10(f) Self-determination.

The resident has the right to and the facility must promote and facilitate resident self- determination through support of resident choice, including but not limited to the rights specified in paragraphs (f)(1) through (11) of this section.

§483.10(f)(1) The resident has a right to choose activities, schedules *(including sleeping and waking times),* health care and *providers of health care services* consistent with his or her interests, assessments, and plan of care and *other applicable provisions of this part.*

§483.10(f)(2) The resident has a right to make choices about aspects of his or her life in the facility that are significant to the resident.

§483.10(f)(3) The resident has a right to interact with members of the community *and participate in community activities* both inside and outside the facility.

§483.10(f)(8) The resident has a right to participate in other activities, including social, religious, and community activities that do not interfere with the rights of other residents in the facility.

GUIDANCE: EXERPTS FROM THE SURVEYOR'S GUIDELINES §483.10(f)(1)-(3), (8)

It is important for residents to have a choice *about which activities they* participate in, whether they are part of the formal activities program or self-directed. *Additionally, a resident's needs and choices for how he or she spends time, both inside and outside the facility, should also be supported and accommodated, to the extent possible, including making transportation arrangements.*

Residents have the right to **choose** their schedules, consistent with their interests, assessments, and **care** plans. **This** includes, but is not limited to, choices **about** the schedules that are important to the resident, such as waking, eating, bathing, and going to bed at night. **Choices about schedules and ensuring that residents are able to get enough sleep is an important contributor to overall health and well-being.** Residents **also** have the right to choose health care schedules consistent with their interests and preferences, and **information** should be gathered **to proactively assist residents with the fulfillment of their choices. Facilities must not develop a schedule for care, such as waking or bathing schedules, for staff convenience and without the input of the residents.**

Examples that demonstrate the support and accommodation of resident goals, preferences, and choices include, but are not limited to:

- *If a resident shares that attendance at family gatherings or external community events is of interest to them, the resident's goals of attending these events should be accommodated, to the extent possible.*
- *If a resident mentions that his or her therapy is scheduled at the time of a favorite television program, the resident's preference should be accommodated, to the extent possible.*
- *If a resident refuses a bath because he or she prefers a shower or a different bathing method, such as in-bed bathing, prefers to bathe at a different time of day or on a different day, does not feel well that day, is uneasy about the aide assigned to help or is worried about falling, the resident's preferences must be accommodated.*

###

F562—Immediate Access to Resident

FOR VOICES FOR QUALITY CARE ADVOCATES

The person living in the nursing home determines who will visit them and when.

This has been an ongoing battle for Voices Volunteers since the organization was founded. This federal regulation was passed in 1987. By now, this should be standard procedure in all U.S. nursing homes. Unfortunately, it is not.

We still encounter signage in nursing home lobbies stating specific visiting hours giving the impression that these are the only times visitors are allowed. These signs should be red flags for volunteer advocates and should be reported and addressed.

Equally disturbing are announcements that "visiting hours are ending" with the implication that all visitors should leave the building.

All nursing homes should have a process well known to family members and friends as to how to enter and exit the building when the doors are locked for the night.

THE REGULATIONS

§483.10(f)(4)(i) The facility must provide immediate access to any resident by:

- (A) Any representative of the Secretary,
- (B(Any representative of the State,
- *(C) Any representative of the Office of the* State long term care ombudsman, (established under section 712 of the Older Americans Act of 1965, *as amended 2016 (42 U.S.C. 3001 et seq.),*
- (D) The resident's individual physician,
- *(E) Any representative of the* protection and advocacy systems, *as designated by the state, and as* established under the

Developmental Disabilities Assistance and Bill of Rights Act *of 2000 (42 U.S.C. 15001 et seq),*

- *(F) Any representative of the* agency responsible *for* the protection and advocacy system for individuals with *mental disorder* (established under the Protection and Advocacy for Mentally Ill Individuals Act *of 2000 (42 U.S.C. 10801 et seq.), and*
- *(G) The resident representative*

GUIDANCE: EXERPTS FROM THE SURVEYOR'S GUIDELINES

The facility must provide immediate access to the resident by the resident's physician, representative, and various state and federal officials and organizations as outlined in the regulation, which would include state and federal surveyors.

Surveyors are considered representatives of the Secretary and/or the State. Facility staff cannot prohibit surveyors from talking to residents, family members, and resident representatives.

NOTE: If facility staff attempt to interfere with the survey process and restrict a surveyor's ability to gather necessary information to determine compliance with requirements, surveyors should consult with the CMS Regional Office.

F563—Right to Receive/Deny Visitors

FOR VOICES FOR QUALITY CARE ADVOCATES

The person living in the nursing home determines who will visit them and when.

Be certain a nursing home allows access to friends and families of residents whenever they wish to visit. Be aware also that when an advocate visits a person living in a nursing home, they are entitled to privacy for that meeting.

This has been an ongoing battle for Voices Volunteers since the organization was founded. This federal regulation was passed in 1987. By now, this should be standard procedure in all U.S. nursing homes. Unfortunately, it is not.

We still encounter signage in nursing home lobbies stating specific visiting hours giving the impression that these are the only times visitors are allowed. These signs should be red flags for volunteer advocates and should be reported and addressed.

Equally disturbing are announcements that "visiting hours are ending" with the implication that all visitors should leave the building.

All nursing homes should have a written visitation policy well known to family members and friends who might visit as to how to enter and exit the building when the doors are locked for the night.

THE REGULATIONS

§483.10(f)(4) The resident has a right to receive visitors of his or her choosing at the time of his or her choosing, subject to the resident's right to deny visitation when applicable, and in a manner that does not impose on the rights of another resident.

- *(ii) The facility must provide immediate access to a resident by* immediate family and other relatives of the resident,

48

subject to the resident's right to deny or withdraw consent at any time;

- *(iii)The facility must provide immediate access to a resident by others who are visiting with the consent of the resident*, subject to reasonable *clinical and safety* restrictions and the resident's right to deny or withdraw consent at any time;

- *(iv)* The facility must provide reasonable access to a resident by any entity or individual that provides health, social, legal, or other services to the resident, subject to the resident's right to deny or withdraw consent at any time; *and*

- *(v) The facility must have written policies and procedures regarding the visitation rights of residents, including those setting forth any clinically necessary or reasonable restriction or limitation or safety restriction or limitation, when such limitations may apply consistent with the requirements of this subpart, that the facility may need to place on such rights and the reasons for the clinical or safety restriction or limitation.*

DEFINITIONS

DEFINITIONS §483.10(f)(4)(ii)-(v)

"Reasonable *clinical and safety* restrictions"

*include a facility's policies, procedures or practices that protect the **health and** security of all residents **and staff. These may include, but are not be limited to:***

- *Restrictions placed to prevent community-associated infection or communicable disease transmission to the resident. A resident's risk factors for infection (e.g., immunocompromised condition) or current health state (e.g., end-of-life care) should be considered when restricting visitors. In general, visitors with signs and symptoms of a transmissible infection (e.g., a visitor is febrile and exhibiting signs and symptoms of an influenza-like illness) should defer visitation until he or she is no longer potentially infectious (e.g., 24 hours after resolution of fever without antipyretic medication). If deferral cannot occur such as the case of end-of-life, the visitor should follow respiratory hygiene/cough etiquette as well as other infection prevention and control practices such as appropriate hand hygiene.*

- Keeping the facility locked *or secured* at night *with a system in place for allowing visitors approved by the resident;*

- Denying access or providing limited and supervised access to an individual if that individual *is suspected of abusing, exploiting, or coercing a resident until an investigation into the allegation has been completed or* has been *found* to be abusing, exploiting, or coercing a resident;

- Denying access to individuals who have been found to have been committing criminal acts such as theft; or

- Denying access to individuals who are inebriated *or* disruptive.

GUIDANCE: EXERPTS FROM THE SURVEYOR'S GUIDELINES §483.10(f)(4)(ii)-(v)

For purposes of this regulation, immediate family is not restricted to individuals united by blood, adoptive, or marital ties, or a State's common law equivalent. It is important to understand that there are many types of families, each of which being equally viable as a supportive, caring unit. For example, it might also include a foster family where one or more adult serves as a temporary guardian for one or more children to whom they may or may not be biologically related. Residents have the right to define their family. During the admissions process, facility staff should discuss this issue with the resident. If the resident is unable to express or communicate whom they identify as family, facility staff should discuss this with the resident's representative.

Resident's family members are not subject to visiting hour limitations or other restrictions **not imposed by the resident**. With the consent of the resident, facilities must provide 24-hour access to other non-relative visitors, *subject to reasonable clinical and safety restrictions*.

If these visitation rights infringe upon the rights of other residents, facility staff must find a location other than a resident's room for visits. For example, if a resident's family visits in the late evening when the resident's roommate is asleep, then the visit should take place somewhere other than their shared room so that the roommate is not disturbed.

Individuals who provide health, social, legal, or other services to the resident have the right of reasonable access to the resident. Facility *staff must provide space and privacy for such visits.*

Examples of noncompliance may include, but are not limited to:

- *Facility staff restrict visitors according to the facility's convenience.*
- *Facility staff restrict the rights of a resident to receive visitors, even though this would not affect the rights of other residents.*
- *Facility staff restrict visitors based on expressed wishes of an individual who is a health care power of attorney who does not have the authority to restrict visitation.*
- *A posting or inclusion in the resident handbook or other information provided by the facility, of visiting hours not in compliance with this regulation.*

###

F564—Inform of Visitation Rights/Equal Visitation

THE REGULATIONS

§483.10(f)(4)(vi) A facility must meet the following requirements:

- *(A) Inform each resident (or resident representative, where appropriate) of his or her visitation rights and related facility policy and procedures, including any clinical or safety restriction or limitation on such rights, consistent with the requirements of this subpart, the reasons for the restriction or limitation, and to whom the restrictions apply, when he or she is informed of his or her other rights under this section.*

- *(B) Inform each resident of the right, subject to his or her consent, to receive the visitors whom he or she designates, including, but not limited to, a spouse (including a same- sex spouse), a domestic partner (including a same-sex domestic partner), another family member, or a friend, and his or her right to withdraw or deny such consent at any time.*

- *(C) Not restrict, limit, or otherwise deny visitation privileges on the basis of race, color, national origin, religion, sex, gender identity, sexual orientation, or disability.*

- *(D) Ensure that all visitors enjoy full and equal visitation privileges consistent with resident preferences.*

<u>*Examples of noncompliance may include, but are not limited to:*</u>

- *Prohibiting a resident from having visits from his or her spouse or domestic partner, including a same-sex spouse or partner.*

- *Facility staff did not inform a resident, the family, and/or resident representative of their visitation rights, including any restrictions or limitations of these rights that may be imposed by the facility or the resident, the family, and/or resident representative;*
- *Facility staff denied, limited or restricted a resident's visitation privileges contrary to their choices, even though there were no clinical or safety reasons for doing so.*

###

F565—Resident/Family Group and Response

FOR VOICES FOR QUALITY CARE ADVOCATES

For Family Council advocacy in Maryland, be aware that Voices has been instrumental in the passage of the Maryland Family Council Law which gives additional rights to Family Councils in Maryland. **For Family Councils operating in both nursing homes and assisted living facilities** in Montgomery County, Maryland, a county ordinance also guarantees these rights. The State Law and County Ordinance are included at the end of this F-Tag section.

THE REGULATIONS

§483.10(f)(5) The resident has a right to organize and participate in resident groups in the facility.

- *(i)* The facility must provide a resident or family group, if one exists, with private space; *and take reasonable steps, with the approval of the group, to make residents and family members aware of upcoming meetings in a timely manner.*
- *(ii)* Staff, visitors, *or other guests* may attend *resident group or family group* meetings *only* at the *respective* group's invitation.
- *(iii)* The facility must provide a designated staff person *who is approved by the resident or family group and the facility and who is* responsible for providing assistance and responding to written requests that result from group meetings.
- *(iv) The facility* must *consider* the views *of a resident or family group* and act *promptly* upon the grievances and recommendations *of such groups* concerning *issues of* resident care and life in the facility.
  - ○ *(A) The facility must be able to demonstrate their response and rationale for such response.*

54

○ *(B) This should not be construed to mean that the facility must implement as recommended every request of the resident or family group.*

§483.10(f)(6) The resident has a right to participate in family groups.

§483.10(f)(7) The resident has a right to have family **member(s) or other resident representative(s)** meet in the facility with the families **or resident representative(s)** of other residents in the facility.

DEFINITIONS §483.10(f)(5)-(7)

<u>"A resident or family group"</u> is defined as a group of residents or residents' family members that meets regularly to:

- *Discuss and offer suggestions about facility policies and procedures affecting residents' care, treatment, and quality of life;*

- *Support each other;*

- *Plan resident and family activities;*

- *Participate in educational activities; or*

- *For any other purpose*

- *Examples of noncompliance may include, but are not limited to:*

- *Facility staff impede or prevent residents or family members ability to meet or organize a resident or family group;*

- *Resident and/or families were not always informed in advance of upcoming meetings.*

- *Facility staff impede with meetings and/or operations of family or resident council by mandating that they have a staff person in the room during meetings or assigning a staff person to liaise with the council that is not agreeable to the council;*

- *Private meeting space for these groups is not provided;*

- *The views, grievances or recommendations from these groups have not been considered or acted upon by facility staff;*

- Facility staff does not provide these groups with responses, actions, and rationale taken regarding their concerns

GUIDANCE: EXERPTS FROM THE SURVEYOR'S GUIDELINES

Examples of noncompliance may include, but are not limited to:

- *Facility staff impede or prevent residents or family members ability to meet or organize a resident or family group;*
- *Resident and/or families were not always informed in advance of upcoming meetings.*
- *Facility staff impede with meetings and/or operations of family or resident council by mandating that they have a staff person in the room during meetings or assigning a staff person to liaise with the council that is not agreeable to the council;*
- *Private meeting space for these groups is not provided;*
- *The views, grievances or recommendations from these groups have not been considered or acted upon by facility staff;*
- *Facility staff does not provide these groups with responses, actions, and rationale taken regarding their concerns*

56

Maryland Family Council Statute

Article— Health — General § 19-1416.

(a) In this section, "family council" means a group of individuals who work together to protect the rights of and improve the quality of life of residents of a nursing home.

(b) (1) A family council for a nursing home may consist of the following members:

(i) Members of a resident's family; or

(ii) An individual appointed by the resident, or if the resident is incapable of appointing an individual, an individual appointed by the resident's family.

(2)

(i) Subject to subparagraph (ii) of this paragraph, a family council may be created by the owner, operator, or staff of a nursing home.

(ii) Except as provided in paragraph (3) of this subsection, in order to facilitate the development of a family council, the owner, operator, or staff of a nursing home may lead the family council for no longer than 6 months at which time the family council shall be led by a member of the family council.

(3) On the written request of a family council, the nursing home may assist the family council in the administrative functions of operating the family council in a mutually agreed upon manner.

(c) A nursing home shall give each new or prospective resident the following written information about the family council:

(1) The name, address, and phone number of a current member of the family council;

(2) A brief description of the purpose and function of the family council;

(3) Instructions on how the resident or prospective resident may review the public files described in subsection (e) of this section; and

(4) The name, address, and phone number of the State or local ombudsman.

(d) A nursing home shall respond in writing to any written grievance or other written communication from the family council within 14 calendar days after receiving a communication.

(e)   (1) A nursing home shall create and maintain a public correspondence file and a regulatory correspondence file for communications with a family council.

(2) The correspondence files shall include a copy of each written communication and response described in subsection (d) of this section.

(3)   (i) The records in the regulatory file shall be unedited.

(ii) The records in the public file shall delete any information that identifies an individual resident.

(4) The public file may be reviewed by a resident, prospective resident, or the representative of either a resident or prospective resident during normal business hours and at any other time the nursing home agrees to make the public file available.

(5) The nursing home shall promptly comply with a request by a licensing authority to review the records in either the public or regulatory files

==========

Legal Code of Montgomery County

Bill No. 35-02

Introduced: October 22, 2002

Revised: Nov. 26, 2002

Enacted: November 26, 2002

Effective: March 6, 2003

Sec. 25-1. Definitions.

For the purposes of this Chapter, the following words and phrases have the following meanings:

Family council: A group that includes a family member, friend, or representative of 2 or more residents of a nursing home or other facility subject to Section 25-24A. A family council is led by residents and their families, not by the facility, and works to protect residents rights and improve residents quality of life.

Sec. 25-24. Application of article.

This Article applies to hospitals, nursing homes, personal care homes and domiciliary care homes. State and federal law and regulations that apply to these institutions, except licensing procedures, are incorporated into this Article. The other provisions of this Article apply only to the extent that they impose higher standards or stricter requirements than State and federal law and regulations. (Mont. Co. Code 1965, § 89-23; Ord. No. 6-18, §2; 2002 L.M.C., ch. 36, § 1.)

Sec. 25-24A. Family councils.

- *(a) In this Section, "nursing home" includes nursing homes (as defined in Section 25-1) and any other facility in the County that is:*
-
  o *(1) required to be licensed under State law as a:*
    - *(A) comprehensive and extended care facility; or*
    - *(B) licensed assisted living facility; or*
  o *(2) subject to sections 1395i-3 or 1396r of Title 42 of the United States Code.*
- *(b) Each nursing home must comply with federal law and regulations, including the Nursing Home Reform Act of 1987, that protect the rights of residents and their families and representatives to associate and to participate in resident and family groups, such as a family council. This requirement applies even if the nursing home is not otherwise subject to the federal law.*
- *(c) The nursing home must consider and respond in writing to any written grievance or other written communication from a family council within 10 days after receiving the communication.*

- *(d) The nursing home must maintain a "regulatory" file and a "public" file containing duplicate copies of each communication and response described in subsection (c). Copies of the records in the regulatory file must be complete and unedited. The same records in the public file must delete any information that identifies an individual resident.*
  - *(1) A resident or prospective resident, or any person representing either, may review the public file during normal business hours and at any other time that the nursing home agrees to make the file available.*
  - *(2) The nursing home promptly must comply with a request by a licensing authority or the County's Long term Care Ombudsman to review any record in either file.*
- *(e) The nursing home must give each new or prospective resident the following written information provided by the family council:*
  - *(1) the name, address, and phone number of a current member of the family council;*

  - *(2) a brief description of the purpose and function of the family council; and*
  - *(3) instructions on how the resident or prospective resident may review the files described in subsection (d). (2002 L.M.C., ch. 36, § 1.)*
  - *Sec. 25-25. Approval of establishment.*

Additional:

(f) A family council may include additional categories of members if the members of the family council agree to expand eligibility for membership and find that the additional members would promote the purposes of the family council.

# # #

F566—Right to Perform Facility Services or Refuse

FOR VOICES FOR QUALITY CARE ADVOCATES

A Desire to Work Should Be Encouraged

Boredom is one of the worst aspects of life in a nursing home. In some cases, a work assignment can be the difference between continual monotony and an interesting life.

THE REGULATIONS

§483.10(f)(9) The resident has a right to choose or refuse to perform services for the facility *and the facility must not require a resident to perform services for the facility. The resident may* perform services for the facility, if he or she chooses, when—

- (i) The facility has documented the resident's need or desire for work in the plan of care;
- (ii) The plan specifies the nature of the services performed and whether the services are voluntary or paid;
- (iii) Compensation for paid services is at or above prevailing rates; and
- (iv) The resident agrees to the work arrangement described in the plan of care.

DEFINITIONS §483.10(f)(9)

"Prevailing rate"

is the wage paid to the majority of workers in the community surrounding the facility for the same type, quality, and quantity of work requiring comparable skills.

###

F567— Protection/Management of Personal Funds

FOR VOICES FOR QUALITY CARE ADVOCATES

All Residents and/or their Representatives have the right to manage their own finances if they choose to do so. Voices Volunteers have encountered a number of nursing home administrative staffs that have insisted that the nursing home financial department must handle all funds. This violates both state and federal regulations and must be corrected.

THE REGULATIONS

§483.10(f)(10) The resident has a right to manage his or her financial affairs. *This includes the right to know, in advance, what charges a facility may impose against a resident's personal funds.*

- *(i)* The facility *must* not require residents to deposit their personal funds with the facility. *If a resident chooses to deposit personal funds with the facility*, upon written authorization of a resident, *the facility must act as a fiduciary of the resident's funds and* hold, safeguard, manage, and account for the personal funds of the resident deposited with the facility, as specified in *this section.*
- *(ii)* Deposit of Funds.
  - *(A) In general: Except as set out in paragraph (f)(lo)(ii)(B) of this section*, the facility must deposit any residents' personal funds in excess of *$100* in an interest bearing account (or accounts) that is separate from any of the facility's operating accounts, and that credits all interest earned on resident's funds to that account. (In pooled accounts, there must be a separate accounting for each resident's share.) The facility must maintain a resident's personal funds that do not exceed

$100 in a non-interest bearing account, interest-bearing account, or petty cash fund.

○ *(B) Residents whose care is funded by Medicaid: The facility must deposit the residents' personal funds in excess of $50 in an interest bearing account (or accounts) that is separate from any of the facility's operating accounts, and that credits all interest earned on resident's funds to that account. (In pooled accounts, there must be a separate accounting for each resident's share.) The facility must maintain personal funds that do not exceed $50 in a noninterest bearing account, interest-bearing account, or petty cash fund.*

INTENT §483.10(f)(10)(i)-(ii)

To assure residents who have authorized the facility in writing to manage any personal funds have ready and reasonable access to those funds.

DEFINITIONS §483.10(f)(10)(i)-(ii)

"Hold, safeguard, manage, and account for"

means that the facility must act as fiduciary of the resident's funds and report at least quarterly on the status of these funds in a clear and understandable manner. Managing the resident's financial affairs includes money that an individual gives to the facility for the sake of providing a resident with a non-covered service. In these instances, the facility will provide a receipt to the gift giver and retain a copy.

"Interest bearing"

means a rate of return equal to or above the rate at local banking institutions in the area. If pooled accounts are used, interest must be prorated per individual on the basis of actual earnings or end-of quarter balance.

GUIDANCE: EXERPTS FROM THE SURVEYOR'S GUIDELINES §483.10(f)(10)(i)-(ii)

If a resident or resident representative chooses to have the facility manage the resident's funds, facility staff may not refuse to handle these funds. *Facility staff are* not expected to be familiar with resident assets not on deposit with the facility.

Residents should have access to petty cash on an ongoing basis and be able to arrange for access to larger funds. Although the facility need not maintain *$100.00 ($50.00 for Medicaid residents)* per resident on its premises, it is expected to maintain petty cash on hand *to honor resident requests.*

Resident requests for access to their funds should be honored by facility *staff as soon as possible but no later than*:

- The same day for amounts less than *$100.00 ($50.00 for Medicaid residents);*
- Three banking days for amounts *of $100.00 ($50.00 for Medicaid residents)* or more.

Residents may make requests that the facility temporarily place their funds in a safe place, without authorizing the facility to manage those funds. *The facility must have a system to document the date, time, amount, and who the funds were received from or dispersed to.*

The facility *must have systems in place to safeguard against any* misappropriation of a *resident's* funds.

NOTE: Banks may charge the resident a fee for handling their funds *and pass this fee on to the resident(s).* Facilities may not charge residents for managing residents' funds because the services are covered by Medicare or Medicaid or by the facility's per diem rate. Monies due residents should be credited to their respective bank accounts within a few business days.

#

F568— Accounting and Records of Personal Funds

FOR VOICES FOR QUALITY CARE ADVOCATES

Accounting is an issue that often comes up in cases where there is a question regarding the finances of a nursing home resident. It is appropriate here, with a signed Permission to Advocate form, to request a full resident's statement from the nursing home finance department in order to determine whether or not finances are being properly handled and disbursed. Determine whether or not the facility is accounting for all funds and whether or not proper receipts and quarterly statements have been provided as required.

THE REGULATIONS

§483.10(f)(10)(iii) Accounting and Records.

- *(A)* The facility must establish and maintain a system that assures a full and complete and separate accounting, according to generally accepted accounting principles, of each resident's personal funds entrusted to the facility on the resident's behalf.
- *(B)* The system must preclude any commingling of resident funds with facility funds or with the funds of any person other than another resident.
- *(C)* The individual financial record must be available *to the resident* through quarterly statements and upon request.

GUIDANCE: EXERPTS FROM THE SURVEYOR'S GUIDELINES

Generally accepted accounting *principles* means that facility *staff* employ proper bookkeeping techniques, by which it can determine, upon request, the amount of individual resident funds and, in the case of an interest bearing account, how much interest these funds have earned for each resident, as last reported by the banking institution to the facility.

Proper bookkeeping techniques include an individual **record** established for each resident on which only those transactions involving his or her personal funds are recorded and maintained.

The record should have information on when transactions occurred, what they were, and maintain the ongoing balance for every resident. For each transaction, the resident should be given a receipt and the facility retains a copy.

Quarterly statements **must** be provided in writing to the resident or the resident's representative within 30 days after the end of the quarter, and upon request.

F569— Notice and Conveyance of Personal Funds

THE REGULATIONS

§483.10(f)(10)(iv) Notice of certain balances.

The facility must notify each resident that receives Medicaid benefits—

- *(A)* When the amount in the resident's account reaches $200 less than the SSI resource limit for one person, specified in section 1611(a)(3)(B) of the Act; and
- *(B)* That, if the amount in the account, in addition to the value of the resident's other nonexempt resources, reaches the SSI resource limit for one person, the resident may lose eligibility for Medicaid or SSI.

§483.10(f)(10)(v) Conveyance upon discharge, eviction, or death.

Upon the *discharge, eviction, or* death of a resident with a personal fund deposited with the facility, the facility must convey within 30 days the resident's funds, and a final accounting of those funds, to the resident, or in the case of death, the individual or probate jurisdiction administering the resident's estate, *in accordance with State law*.

###

F570—(Omitted)Surety Bond - Security of Personal Funds

For information on this Regulation see the Surveyor's Guidelines

F571—Limitations on Charges to Personal Funds

FOR VOICES FOR QUALITY CARE ADVOCATES

This is a rather important regulation. Some facilities have attempted to bill Residents for lapses in Medicaid coverage due to late paperwork submissions by the nursing home or the late processing of applications by the state Medicaid agency. Occasionally facilities have billed for services covered by Medicaid or Medicare. Review the resident's financial statements for complaints of this nature.

THE REGULATIONS

§483.10(f)(11) The facility *must* not impose a charge against the personal funds of a resident for any item or service for which payment is made under Medicaid or Medicare (except for applicable deductible and coinsurance amounts).

The facility may charge the resident for requested services that are more expensive than or in excess of covered services in accordance with §489.32 of this chapter. (This does not affect the prohibition on facility charges for items and services for which Medicaid has paid. See §447.15 of this chapter, which limits participation in the Medicaid program to providers who accept, as payment in full, Medicaid payment plus any deductible, coinsurance, or copayment required by the plan to be paid by the individual.)

- (i) Services included in Medicare or Medicaid payment. During the course of a covered Medicare or Medicaid stay, facilities *must* not charge a resident for the following categories of items and services:
    - (A) Nursing services as required at §483.35.
    - *(B) Food and Nutrition services as required at §483.60.*
    - (C) An activities program as required at §483.24(c).
    - (D) Room/bed maintenance services.
    - (E) Routine personal hygiene items and services as required to meet the needs of residents, including, but not limited to, hair

68

hygiene supplies, comb, brush, bath soap, disinfecting soaps or specialized cleansing agents when indicated to treat special skin problems or to fight infection, razor, shaving cream, toothbrush, toothpaste, denture adhesive, denture cleaner, dental floss, moisturizing lotion, tissues, cotton balls, cotton swabs, deodorant, incontinence care and supplies, sanitary napkins and related supplies, towels, washcloths, hospital gowns, over the counter drugs, hair and nail hygiene services, bathing **assistance**, and basic personal laundry.

  o (F) Medically-related social services as required at *§483.40(d).*

  o *(G) Hospice services elected by the resident and paid for under the Medicare Hospice Benefit or paid for by Medicaid under a state plan.*

- (ii) Items and services that may be charged to residents' funds. *Paragraphs (f)(11)(ii)(A) through (L) of this* section are general categories and examples of items and services that the facility may charge to residents' funds if they are requested by a resident, *if they are not required to achieve the goals stated in the resident's care plan,* if the facility informs the resident that there will be a charge, and if payment is not made by Medicare or Medicaid:

  o (A) Telephone, *including a cellular phone.*

  o (B) Television/radio, *personal computer or other electronic device* for personal use.

  o (C) Personal comfort items, including smoking materials, notions and novelties, and confections.

  o (D) Cosmetic and grooming items and services in excess of those for which payment is made under Medicaid or Medicare.

  o (E) Personal clothing.

  o (F) Personal reading matter.

  o (G) Gifts purchased on behalf of a resident.

  o (H) Flowers and plants.

  o (I) *Cost to participate* in social events and entertainment outside the scope of the activities program, provided under *§483.24(c).*

o (J) Non-covered special care services such as privately hired nurses or aides.

o (K) Private room, except when therapeutically required (for example, isolation for infection control).

o *(L) Except as provided in (e)(11)(ii)(L)(1) and (2) of this section*, specially prepared or alternative food requested instead of the food *and meals* generally prepared by the facility, as required by *§483.60.*

- *(1) The facility may not charge for special foods and meals, including medically prescribed dietary supplements, ordered by the resident's physician, physician assistant, nurse practitioner, or clinical nurse specialist, as these are included per §483.60.*

- *(2) In accordance with §483.60(c) through (f), when preparing foods and meals, a facility must take into consideration residents' needs and preferences and the overall cultural and religious make-up of the facility's population.*

• (iii) Requests for items and services.

o (A) The facility *can only* charge a resident for any *non-cov*ered item or service *if such item or service is specifically requested by the resident.*

o (B) The facility must not require a resident to request any item or service as a condition of admission or continued stay.

o (C) The facility must inform, *orally and in writing*, the resident requesting an item or service for which a charge will be made that there will be a charge for the item or service and what the charge will be.

GUIDANCE: EXERPTS FROM THE SURVEYOR'S GUIDELINES §483.10(f)(11)

Residents must not be charged for universal items such as *computers, telephones, television services or other electronic devices, books, magazines* or newspaper subscriptions intended for use by *all residents.*

###

F572—Notice of Rights and Rules

FOR VOICES FOR QUALITY CARE ADVOCATES

When questions regarding Resident Rights come up, do check to be certain that the Resident and the Resident's Representative, if any, have been informed of these Rights and have copies of them. It is also wise when a guardian has been appointed by a court to ensure that the guardian is aware of these Rights and will insist on them.

THE REGULATIONS

§483.10(g) Information and Communication.

§483.10(g)(1) The resident has the right to be informed of his or her rights and of all rules and regulations governing resident conduct and responsibilities during *his or her* stay in the facility.

§483.10(g)(16) The facility must provide a notice of rights and services to the resident prior to or upon admission and during the resident's stay.

- *(i)* The facility must inform the resident both orally and in writing in a language that the resident understands of his or her rights and all rules and regulations governing resident conduct and responsibilities during the stay in the facility.
- *(ii)* The facility must also provide the resident with the State-developed notice of *Medicaid rights and obligations, if any*.
- *(iii)* Receipt of such information, and any amendments to it, must be acknowledged in writing;

INTENT §483.10(g)(1),(16)

This requirement is intended to assure that each resident knows his or her rights and responsibilities and that facility staff communicates this information prior to or upon admission, as appropriate during the resident's stay, and when the facility's rules change.

DEFINITIONS §483.10(g)(1),(16)

"All rules and regulations"

relates to State and Federal requirements and facility policies.

"Both orally and in writing"

means if a resident can read and understand written materials without assistance, an oral summary, along with the written document, is acceptable.

"In a language that the resident understands"

means verbally, in writing, and in a language that is clear and understandable to the resident and/or his or her representative.

GUIDANCE: EXERPTS FROM THE SURVEYOR'S GUIDELINES §483.10(g)(1),(16)

Any time State or Federal laws *or regulations* relating to resident rights or facility *policies* change during the resident's stay in the facility, he/she must promptly be informed of these changes *in a manner that is clear to the resident.*

A resident cannot be expected to abide by rules he/she has never been told about. Whatever rules *or policies* the facility has formalized, and by which it expects residents to abide, should be included in the *residents'* statement of rights and responsibilities.

If a resident *or his/her representative's understanding* of English or the predominant language of the facility is inadequate for *their* comprehension, a means to communicate information in a language *or format* familiar to the resident *or his/her representative* must *be used.* The facility *must* have written translations, *including Braille*, and make the services of an interpreter available *as needed.* For those residents *who* communicate in American Sign Language (ASL), facility *staff are* expected to provide an interpreter. Large print texts of the facility's statement of resident rights and responsibilities *may* also be made available.

F573— Right to Access/Purchase Copies of Records

FOR VOICES FOR QUALITY CARE ADVOCATES

This regulation was first passed in 1987, yet in many facilities in numerous states, requests to view or obtain copies of parts or all of a resident's records are met with negative responses. In Maryland, the Office of Health Care Quality has communicated to nursing homes written instructions on how to implement the right to access and receive all resident records including digitalized records where they exist. Where such a request is not met immediately with a positive response, contact the Voices email or toll-free phone

THE REGULATIONS

§483.10(g)(2) The resident has the right to access personal and medical records pertaining to him or herself.

- (i) *The facility must provide the resident* with access to personal and medical records pertaining to him or herself, upon an oral or written request, *in the form and format requested by the individual, if it is readily producible in such form and format (including in an electronic form or format when such records are maintained electronically), or, if not, in a readable hard copy form or such other form and format as agreed to by the facility and the individual,* within 24 hours (excluding weekends and holidays); and

- (ii) *The facility must allow the resident to obtain a copy of the records or any portions thereof (including in an electronic form or format when such records are maintained electronically)* upon request and 2 working days advance notice to the facility. *The facility may impose a reasonable, cost-based fee on the provision of copies, provided that the fee includes only the cost of:*
  - ○ *(A) Labor for copying the records requested by the individual, whether in paper or electronic form;*

74

○ *(B) Supplies for creating the paper copy or electronic media if the individual requests that the electronic copy be provided on portable media; and*

○ *(C) Postage, when the individual has requested the copy be mailed.*

§483.10*(g)(3) With the exception of information described in paragraphs (g)(2) and (g)(11) of this section, the facility must ensure that information is provided to each resident in a form and manner the resident can access and understand, including in an alternative format or in a language that the resident can understand. Summaries that translate information described in paragraph (g)(2) of this section may be made available to the patient at their request and expense in accordance with applicable law.*

DEFINITIONS §483.10(g)(2)-(3)

"Records,"

includes all records, in addition to clinical records, pertaining to the resident, such as trust fund ledgers pertinent to the resident and contracts between the resident and the facility.

GUIDANCE: EXERPTS FROM THE SURVEYOR'S GUIDELINES §483.10(g)(2)-(3)

An oral request is sufficient to produce *the resident's personal and medical* record for review.

The facility may charge a reasonable, cost-based fee for providing a copy of the requested records, whether in paper or electronic form. This may only include the cost of labor for copying the records, supplies for creating the paper copy or electronic media, and postage, if applicable. Additional fees for locating the records or typing forms/envelopes may not be assessed.

KEY ELEMENTS OF NONCOMPLIANCE §483.10(g)(2)-(3)

To cite deficient practice at F573, the surveyor's investigation will generally show that the facility failed to do one or more of the following:

- *Support the resident's right to access his or her own personal and medical records; or*
- *Provide the resident access to his or her personal and medical records within 24 hours (excluding weekends and holidays) of a written request; or*
- *Allow the resident to purchase a copy of his or her personal and medical records upon request and with 2 working days advanced notice; or*
- *Charge a reasonable, cost-based fee, including only the cost of labor, supplies, and postage involved in providing or sending the personal and medical records requested; or*
- *Ensure the information is provided:*
  - *In a form the resident can access and understand ;or*
  - *In a form and format agreed upon by the facility and the resident.*

F574— Required Notices and Contact Information

FOR VOICES FOR QUALITY CARE ADVOCATES

Contact information for agencies acting on behalf of residents is often posted but no one uses it. Many people living in nursing homes and their friends and families are reluctant to use this information and make the call for fear that simply doing so might in some way anger or alter their current relationship with facility staff. If only one person makes use of this information, it well might. But, if most of the people visiting or living in the nursing

THE REGULATIONS

§483.10(g)(4) The resident has the right to receive notices orally (meaning spoken) and in writing (including Braille) in a format and a language he or she understands, including:

- *(i) Required notices as specified in this section.* The facility must furnish to each resident a written description of legal rights which includes –
  - *(A)* A description of the manner of protecting personal funds, under paragraph *(f)(10)* of this section;
  - *(B)* A description of the requirements and procedures for establishing eligibility for Medicaid, including the right to request an assessment *of resources* under section 1924(c) *of the Social Security Act.*
  - *(C) A list of* names, addresses *(mailing and email)*, and telephone numbers of all pertinent State *regulatory and informational agencies, resident* advocacy groups such as the State Survey Agency, the State licensure office, the State *Long-Term Care O*mbudsman program, the protection and advocacy agency, *adult protective services where state law provides for jurisdiction in long-term care facilities, the local contact agency for information*

about returning to the community and the Medicaid Fraud Control Unit; and

    ○ *(D)* A statement that the resident may file a complaint with the State *Survey Agency* concerning *any suspected violation of state or federal nursing facility regulations, including but not limited to* resident abuse, neglect, *exploitation*, misappropriation of resident property in the facility, non-compliance with the advance directives requirements *and requests for information regarding returning to the community*.

- *(ii) Information and contact information for State and local advocacy organizations including but not limited to the State Survey Agency, the State Long-Term Care Ombudsman program (established under section 712 of the Older Americans Act of 1965, as amended 2016 (42 U.S.C. 3001 et seq) and the protection and advocacy system (as designated by the state, and as established under the Developmental Disabilities Assistance and Bill of Rights Act of 2000 (42 U.S.C. 15001 et seq.)*

- *(iii) Information regarding Medicare and Medicaid eligibility and coverage;*

- *(iv) Contact information for the Aging and Disability Resource Center (established under Section 202(a)(20)(B)(iii) of the Older Americans Act); or other No Wrong Door Program;*

- *(v) Contact information for the Medicaid Fraud Control Unit; and*

- *(vi) Information and contact information for filing grievances or complaints concerning any suspected violation of state or federal nursing facility regulations, including but not limited to resident abuse, neglect, exploitation, misappropriation of resident property in the facility, non-compliance with the advance directives requirements and requests for information regarding returning to the community*

DEFINITIONS §483.10(g)(4)

"Orally and in writing"

means if a resident can read and understand written materials without assistance, an oral summary, along with the written document, is acceptable.

"In a language he or she understands"

means verbally, in writing (including Braille), and in a language that is clear and understandable to the resident or his or her representative.

GUIDANCE: EXERPTS FROM THE SURVEYOR'S GUIDELINES §483.10(g)(4)

If a resident *or his or her representative's understanding* of English or the predominant language of the facility is inadequate for *their* comprehension, a means to communicate information in a language *or format* familiar to the resident *or his or her representative* must *be used.* The facility *must* have written translations, *including Braille* and make the services of an interpreter available as needed. For those residents *wh*o communicate in American Sign Language (ASL), the facility is expected to provide an interpreter. Large print texts of the facility's statement of resident rights and responsibilities should also be available.

As part of determining Medicaid eligibility, at the time of admission, a married couple has the right to request and have the appropriate State agency assess the couple's resources.

During interviews with residents, their representatives and facility staff determine:

- *When and how information regarding rights and services are communicated; and*
- *If this information was provided in a language and format the resident or representative understood.*

#

F575— Required Postings

FOR VOICES FOR QUALITY CARE ADVOCATES

Contact information for agencies acting on behalf of residents is often posted but no one uses it. Many people living in nursing homes and their friends and families are reluctant to use this information and make the call for fear that simply doing so might in some way anger or alter their current relationship with facility staff. If only one person makes use of this information, it well might. But, if most of the people visiting or living in the nursing home or assisted living facility make use of it, it will become the commonplace event it should be.

THE REGULATIONS

§483.10(g)(5) The facility must post, in a form and manner accessible and understandable to residents, resident representatives:

(i) A list of names, addresses *(mailing and email),* and telephone numbers of all pertinent *State agencies and* advocacy groups, such as the State *Survey Agency*, the State licensure office, *adult protective services where state law provides for jurisdiction in long-term care facilities, the Office of the State Long-Term Care* Ombudsman program, the protection and advocacy network, *home and community based service programs, and* the Medicaid Fraud Control Unit; and

(ii) A statement that the resident may file a complaint with the State *Survey Agency* concerning *any suspected violation of state or federal nursing facility regulation, including but not limited to* resident abuse, neglect, *exploitation*, misappropriation of resident property in the facility, and non-compliance with the advanced directives requirements *(42 CFR part 489 subpart I) and requests for information regarding returning to the community.*

###

F576—Right to Forms of Communication with Privacy

The Voices Position

Telephone Access for Private Conversations

This is a situation that Surveyors often overlook or regard as minor, yet it directly affects the quality of life for many people living in a nursing home or assisted living facility. When a complaint is filed, a Complaint Investigator is often shown a space with a door and phone that is actually used at various times by staff as an office or for some other purpose, maybe even a place to eat lunch. Or, despite claims to the contrary, the room may often be locked or otherwise unavailable to residents wishing to make private phone calls.

THE REGULATIONS

§483.10(g)(6) The resident has the right to have reasonable access to the use of a telephone, *including TTY and TDD services, and a place in the facility* where calls can be made without being overheard. *This includes the right to retain and use a cellular phone at the resident's own expense.*

§483.10(g)(7) The facility must protect and facilitate that resident's right to communicate with individuals and entities within and external to the facility, including reasonable access to:

- (i) A telephone, *including TTY and TDD services;*
- (ii*) The internet, to the extent available to the facility; and*
- (iii) Stationery, postage, writing *implements and the ability to send mail.*

§483.10(g)(8) The resident has the right to send and receive mail, *and to receive letters, packages and other materials delivered to the facility for the resident through a means other than a postal service, including the right to:*

- *(i) Privacy of such communications consistent with this section; and*
- (ii) Access to stationery, postage, and writing implements at the resident's own expense.

§483.10(g)(9) The resident has the right to have reasonable access to and privacy in their use of electronic communications such as email and video communications and for internet research.

- *(i) If the access is available to the facility*
- *(ii) At the resident's expense, if any additional expense is incurred by the facility to provide such access to the resident.*
- *(iii) Such use must comply with State and Federal law.*

DEFINITIONS §483.10(g)(6)-(9)

"Reasonable access"

*means that telephones, **computers and other communication devices are easily** accessible to residents and are adapted to accommodate resident's needs and **abilities,** such as hearing or vision loss*

"TTY (TeleTYpe) and TDD (Telecommunications Device for the Deaf)"

are acronyms used interchangeably to refer to any type of text-based telecommunications equipment used by a person who does not have enough functional hearing to understand speech, even with amplification.

GUIDANCE: EXERPTS FROM THE SURVEYOR'S GUIDELINES §483.10(g)(6)-(9)

Resident access to telephones in staff offices or at nurses' stations **alone** does not meet the provisions of this requirement. Examples of facility accommodations to provide reasonable access to the use of a telephone without being overheard include providing cordless telephones or having telephone jacks in residents' rooms.

The facility is responsible for providing reasonable access to the internet to the extent it is available onsite. Computers in public areas for general use must be located in a manner to protect resident privacy in email, communications, and internet use.

F577— Right to Survey Results/Advocate Agency Info

FOR VOICES FOR QUALITY CARE ADVOCATES

The most recent Survey Reports must be available to residents, their families, and visitors. They must be kept in a place easily identified without the need to ask staff for them. They must be in a format that is easy to access and to read. Advocates should check them in any facilities where they are assisting helpline callers to be certain they are easily available and to familiarize themselves with recently cited deficiencies. These reports can also be found on the CMS Nursing Home Compare website and on ProPublica.

THE REGULATIONS

§483.10(g)*(10)* The resident has the right to-

- *(i)* Examine the results of the most recent survey of the facility conducted by Federal or State surveyors and any plan of correction in effect with respect to the facility; and

- *(ii)* Receive information from agencies acting as client advocates, and be afforded the opportunity to contact these agencies.

§483.10(g)*(11) The facility must--*

- *(i) P*ost in a place readily accessible to residents, *and family members and legal representatives of residents, the results of the most recent survey of the facility.*

- (ii)Have reports *with respect to any* surveys, *certifications, and complaint investigations* made respecting the facility *during the 3 preceding years*, and any plan of correction in effect with respect to the facility, *available for any individual to review upon request; and*

- (iii)Post notice of the *availability of such reports in areas of the facility that are prominent and accessible to the public.*

- *(iv) The facility shall not make available identifying information about complainants or residents.*

DEFINITIONS §483.10(g)(10)-(11)

"Place readily accessible"

is a place (such as a lobby or other area frequented by most residents, visitors or other individuals) where individuals wishing to examine survey results do not have to ask to see them

"Results of the most recent survey"

means the Statement of Deficiencies (Form CMS-2567) and the Statement of Isolated Deficiencies generated by the most recent standard survey and any subsequent extended surveys, and any deficiencies resulting from any subsequent complaint investigation(s).

GUIDANCE: EXERPTS FROM THE SURVEYOR'S GUIDELINES §483.10(g)(10)-(11)

The survey results may not be altered by the facility unless authorized by the State agency.

###

F578— Request/Refuse/Discontinue Treatment;Formulate Adv Directives

FOR VOICES FOR QUALITY CARE ADVOCATES

The most recent Survey Reports must be available to residents, their families, and visitors. They must be kept in a place easily identified without the need to ask staff for them. They must be in a format that is easy to access and to read. Advocates should check them in any facilities where they are assisting helpline callers to be certain they are easily available and to familiarize themselves with recently cited deficiencies. These reports can also be found on the CMS Nursing Home Compare website and on ProPublica.

THE REGULATIONS

§483.10(g)(*10*) The resident has the right to-

- *(i)* Examine the results of the most recent survey of the facility conducted by Federal or State surveyors and any plan of correction in effect with respect to the facility; and
- *(ii)* Receive information from agencies acting as client advocates, and be afforded the opportunity to contact these agencies.

§483.10(g)(*11*) *The facility must--*

- *(i) P*ost in a place readily accessible to residents, *and family members and legal representatives of residents, the results of the most recent survey of the facility.*
- (ii)Have reports *with respect to any* surveys, *certifications, and complaint investigations* made respecting the facility *during the 3 preceding years*, and any plan of correction in effect with respect to the facility, *available for any individual to review upon request; and*
- (iii)Post notice of the *availability of such reports in areas of the facility that are prominent and accessible to the public.*

- **(iv) The facility shall not make available identifying information about complainants or residents.**

DEFINITIONS §483.10(g)(10)-(11)

"Place readily accessible"

is a place (such as a lobby or other area frequented by most residents, visitors or other individuals) where individuals wishing to examine survey results do not have to ask to see them

"Results of the most recent survey"

means the Statement of Deficiencies (Form CMS-2567) and the Statement of Isolated Deficiencies generated by the most recent standard survey and any subsequent extended surveys, and any deficiencies resulting from any subsequent complaint investigation(s).

GUIDANCE: EXERPTS FROM THE SURVEYOR'S GUIDELINES §483.10(g)(10)-(11)

The survey results may not be altered by the facility unless authorized by the State agency.

#

F579— Posting/Notice of Medicare/Medicaid on Admission

THE REGULATIONS

§483.10(g)(13) The facility must display in the facility written information, and provide to residents and applicants for admission, oral and written information about how to apply for and use Medicare and Medicaid benefits, and how to receive refunds for previous payments covered by such benefits.

DEFINITIONS §483.10(g)(13)

"Refunds for previous payments" refers to refunds due as a result of Medicaid and Medicare payments when eligibility has been determined retroactively.

GUIDANCE: EXERPTS FROM THE SURVEYOR'S GUIDELINES §483.10(g)(13)

To fulfill this requirement, facility *staff* may use written materials issued by the State Medicaid agency and the Federal government relating to these benefits. Facilities may fulfill their obligation to orally inform residents or *prospective residents* about how to apply for Medicaid or Medicare by assisting them *in working with* the local Social Security Office or the local unit of the State Medicaid agency. *Simply providing a phone number is not sufficient in assisting resident or the resident representative.* Facilities are not responsible for orally providing detailed information about Medicare and Medicaid eligibility rules

###

F580— Notify of Changes (Injury/Decline/Room, Etc.)

FOR VOICES FOR QUALITY CARE ADVOCATES

This is an issue that unfortunately, often comes to us after the fact. We frequently discover violations when we begin untangling the concerns of a helpline caller whose reason for calling was something else entirely. When a medication or a procedure is involved in a care concern, one of the first questions of the advocate should be, "were you informed before this change occurred?"

Nursing homes and the larger assisted living facilities have large staffs that are on duty at different times of the day and on different days compounding the mechanics involved in notifying residents, families, and representatives.

Among the situations we have encountered where residents and their representatives have not been notified of impending changes or newly existing conditions are:

- death
- falls
- medical tests
- changes in medication
- discontinuation of, or changes in, physical therapy
- development and progression of pressure ulcers
- unusual weight loss/gain
- new bruises or other injuries and plausible explanations of the cause
- changes in food consistency, dietary offerings, supplements,
- introduction of feeding tubes
- delirium

For the Maryland Law covering Notification of Changes in Condition scroll to the bottom of this section

THE REGULATIONS

§483.10(g)(14) Notification of Changes.

- (i) A facility must immediately inform the resident; consult with the resident's physician; and notify, **consistent with his or her authority**, the resident representative(s) when there is—
  - o (A) An accident involving the resident which results in injury and has the potential for requiring physician intervention;
  - o (B) A significant change in the resident's physical, mental, or psychosocial status (**that is**, a deterioration in health, mental, or psychosocial status in either life- threatening conditions or clinical complications);
  - o (C) A need to alter treatment significantly (**that is**, a need to discontinue an existing form of treatment due to adverse consequences, or to commence a new form of treatment); or
  - o (D) A decision to transfer or discharge the resident from the facility as specified in *§483.15(c)(1)(ii).*
- *(ii) When making notification under paragraph (g)(14)(i) of this section, the facility must ensure that all pertinent information specified in §483.15(c)(2) is available and provided upon request to the physician.*
- *(iii)* The facility must also promptly notify the resident and the resident representative, *if any*, when there is—
  - o (A) A change in room or roommate assignment as specified in §483.10(e)(6); or
  - o (B) A change in resident rights under Federal or State law or regulations as specified in paragraph *(e)(10)* of this section.
- *(iv)*The facility must record and periodically update the address *(mailing and email)* and phone number of the resident representative(s).

90

DEFINITIONS §483.10(g)(14)

"A need to alter treatment significantly"

means a need to stop a form of treatment because of adverse consequences (such as an adverse drug reaction), or commence a new form of treatment to deal with a problem (for example, the use of any medical procedure, or therapy that has not been used on that resident before).

GUIDANCE: EXERPTS FROM THE SURVEYOR'S GUIDELINES §483.10(g)(14)

While the regulatory obligation is not limited to these symptoms, physician notification should occur when a resident experiences symptoms such as chest pain, loss of consciousness, or other signs or symptoms of heart attack or stroke that may signify a significant change.

Even when a resident is mentally competent, **his or her** designated **resident representative or family, as appropriate,** should be notified of significant changes in the resident's health status because the resident may not be able to notify them personally, especially in the case of sudden illness or accident.

If the resident is not capable of making decisions, facility staff must contact the designated resident representative, consistent with his or her authority, to make any required decisions, but the resident **must** still be told what is happening to him or her

In the case of the death of a resident, the resident's physician is to be notified immediately **by facility staff** in accordance with State law.

For Advocates in Maryland:

There are not only state regulations reinforcing this right but also a State Notification Law

Maryland Statute

Article —Health — General § 19-1415

- *(a)In this section, "change in condition" means a significant change in the resident's physical, mental, or psychological status including:*
  - *(1) Life threatening conditions such as heart attack or stroke;*
  - *(2) Clinical complications such as:*
    - *(i) Development of a pressure sore;*
    - *(ii) Onset of recurrent periods of delirium;*

###

F582— Medicaid/Medicare Coverage/Liability Notice

THE REGULATIONS

§483.10(g)(17) The facility must--

- (i) Inform each ***Medicaid-eligible*** resident, in writing, at the time of admission to the nursing facility ***and*** when the resident becomes eligible for Medicaid of—
  - o (A) The items and services that are included in nursing facility services under the State plan and for which the resident may not be charged;
  - o (B) Those other items and services that the facility offers and for which the resident may be charged, and the amount of charges for those services; and
- (i) Inform each ***Medicaid-eligible*** resident when changes are made to the items and services specified in *§483.10(g)(17)(*i)(A) and (B) of this section.

§483.10(g)(18) The facility must inform each resident before, or at the time of admission, and periodically during the resident's stay, of services available in the facility and of charges for those services, including any charges for services not covered under Medicare/ Medicaid or by the facility's per diem rate.

- *(i) Where changes in coverage are made to items and services covered by Medicare and/or by the Medicaid State plan, the facility must provide notice to residents of the change as soon as is reasonably possible.*
- *(ii) Where changes are made to charges for other items and services that the facility offers, the facility must inform the resident in writing at least 60 days prior to implementation of the change.*

93

- *(iii) If a resident dies or is hospitalized or is transferred and does not return to the facility, the facility must refund to the resident, resident representative, or estate, as applicable, any deposit or charges already paid, less the facility's per diem rate, for the days the resident actually resided or reserved or retained a bed in the facility, regardless of any minimum stay or discharge notice requirements.*
- *(iv) The facility must refund to the resident or resident representative any and all refunds due the resident within 30 days from the resident's date of discharge from the facility.*
- *(v) The terms of an admission contract by or on behalf of an individual seeking admission to the facility must not conflict with the requirements of these regulations*

DEFINITIONS §483.10(g)(17)-(18)

"Periodically"

means whenever changes are being introduced that will affect the resident's liability and whenever there are changes in services.

GUIDANCE: EXERPTS FROM THE SURVEYOR'S GUIDELINES §483.10(g)(17)-(18)

Residents **must** be told in advance when changes will occur in their bills. Providers must fully inform the resident of services and related changes.

A Medicare beneficiary who requires services upon admission that are not covered under Medicare may be required to submit a deposit provided the notice provisions of §483.10(g)(17) if applicable, are met. *Facility staff must notify residents of services or items that they may be charged for, if they are not required by the resident's care plan, such as hair salon services beyond basic services or incontinence briefs the resident requests per personal preference in lieu of the briefs provided by the facility.* See *§483.10(f)(11)* for those items and services that must be included in payment under skilled nursing and nursing facility benefits.

The facility's responsibility regarding refunds applies to all residents for "any deposit or charges already paid" by a resident during their nursing home stay. For residents residing in a Continuing Care Retirement Community (CCRC) an exception can be considered for those residents who were admitted to the CCRC's nursing home, had deposits and charges related to the CCRC separate from those incurred during the nursing home stay, and who were discharged/transferred from the nursing home back to the same CCRC's independent or assisted living residences.

For Medicare Covered Part A Beneficiaries:

If a SNF believes upon admission or during a resident's stay that Medicare will not pay for skilled nursing or specialized rehabilitative services and the SNF believes that an otherwise covered item or service may be denied as not being reasonable and necessary, facility staff must inform the resident or his or her legal representative in writing why these specific services may not be covered and of the beneficiary's potential liability for payment for the non-covered services.

For more information on this topic refer to the Surveyor's guidelines.

###

F583—Personal Privacy/Confidentiality of Records

FOR VOICES FOR QUALITY CARE ADVOCATES

Residents have the right to speak to Voices Advocates in private without staff members insisting on open doors, entering the room during the conversation for non-essential actions, hanging about outside the resident's door, or hovering about the area in which the conversations is taking place. Should a Voices Advocate encounter a situation where facility staff deliberately make a private conversation difficult, an immediate offer to call or a suggestion that staff call the Director of the Licensing Agency for clarification often quickly resolves the situation. In the District of Columbia, the call might be to the Long-Term Care Ombudsman's Office. For appropriate contacts in such a situation, contact the Voices Officers.

In cases where a resident requests that a family member or friend remain during personal care, facility staff cannot require that family member or friend to leave the room.

THE REGULATIONS

§483.10(h) Privacy and Confidentiality.

The resident has a right to personal privacy and confidentiality of his or her personal and **medical** records.

§483.10(h)(l) Personal privacy includes accommodations, medical treatment, written and telephone communications, personal care, visits, and meetings of family and resident groups, but this does not require the facility to provide a private room for each resident.

§483.10(h)(2) The facility must respect the residents right to personal privacy, including the right to privacy in his or her oral (that is, spoken), written, *and electronic* communications, *including the right* to send and promptly receive unopened mail *and other letters, packages and other materials delivered to the*

facility for the resident, including those delivered through a means other than a postal service.

§483.10(h)(3) The resident has a right to secure and confidential personal and medical records.

- *(i)* The resident **has the right to** refuse the release of personal and **medical** records **except as provided at §483.70(i)(2) or other applicable federal or state laws.**
- (ii) The facility must allow representatives of the **Office of the** State **Long-Term Care** Ombudsman to examine a resident's **medical, social, and administrative** records **in accordance** with State law.

DEFINITIONS §483.10(h)

"Confidentiality"

is defined as safeguarding the content of information including video, audio, or other computer stored information from unauthorized disclosure without the consent of the resident and/or the individual's surrogate or representative. If there is information considered too confidential to place in the record used by all staff, such as the family's financial assets or sensitive medical data, it may be retained in a secure place in the facility, such as a locked cabinet in the administrator's office. The record *must* show the location of this confidential information.

"Promptly"

means delivery of mail or other materials to the resident within 24 hours of delivery by the postal service (including a post office box) and delivery of outgoing mail to the postal service within 24 hours, except when there is no regularly scheduled postal delivery and pick-up service

Right to *personal* privacy"

includes the resident's right to *meet or communicate with whomever they want without being watched or overheard*. Private space may be created flexibly and need not be dedicated solely for visitation purposes.

GUIDANCE: EXERPTS FROM THE SURVEYOR'S GUIDELINES §483.10(h)

Each resident has the right to privacy and confidentiality for all aspects of care and services. A nursing home resident has the right to personal privacy of not only his or her own physical body, but of his or her personal space, including accommodations and personal care.

Residents in nursing homes have varying degrees of physical/psychosocial needs, intellectual disabilities, and/or cognitive impairments. A resident may be dependent on nursing home staff for some or all aspects of care, such as assistance with eating, ambulating, bathing, daily personal hygiene, dressing, and bathroom needs. Only authorized staff directly involved in providing care and services for the resident may be present when care is provided, unless the resident consents to other individuals being present during the delivery of care. During the delivery of personal care and services, staff must remove residents from public view, pull privacy curtains or close doors, *and provide clothing or draping to prevent exposure of body parts.*

Photographs or recordings of a resident and/or his or her private space without the resident's, or designated representative's written consent, is a violation of the resident's right to privacy and confidentiality. Examples include, but are not limited to, staff taking unauthorized photographs of a resident's room or furnishings (which may or may not include the resident), or a resident eating in the dining room, or a resident participating in an activity in the common area. Taking unauthorized photographs or recordings of residents in any state of dress or undress using any type of equipment (for example, cameras, smart phones, and other electronic devices) and/or keeping or distributing them through multimedia messages or on social media networks is a violation of a resident's right to privacy and confidentiality.

Personal and **medical** records include all types of records the facility might keep on a resident, whether they are medical, social, fund accounts, automated, **electronic**, or other. *Care must be taken to protect the privacy of personal information on all residents, including gender identity and sexual orientation.*

Posting signs in residents' rooms or in areas **visible to others** that include clinical or personal **information could be considered a violation of a resident's privacy.** It is allowable to post signs with this type of information in more private locations not **visible to the** public. An exception can be made in an individual case if a resident **or his or her representative requests** the posting of information at the bedside (**such as instructions to** not take blood pressure in right arm). This does not prohibit the display of resident names on their doors nor does it prohibit display of resident memorabilia and/or biographical information in or outside their rooms with their consent or the consent of his or her representative. (This does not include isolation precaution **information** for public health protection, as long as the sign does not reveal the type of infection).

Personal resident information **must be communicated** in a way that protects the confidentiality of the information and the dignity of residents. This includes both verbal and written communications such as **the presence of** lists of residents with certain conditions such as incontinence and pressure ulcers at nursing stations in view or in hearing of residents and visitors. This does not include clinical information written in a resident's record.

Privacy for visitation or meetings might be arranged by using a dining area between meals, a vacant chapel, office or room; or an activities area when activities are not in progress. Arrangements for private space could be accomplished through cooperation between the facility's administration and resident or family groups so that private space is provided for those requesting it without infringement on the rights of other residents.

#

F584—*Safe/Clean/Comfortable/Homelike Environment

FOR VOICES FOR QUALITY CARE ADVOCATES

The state and district regulations on the required lighting in nursing homes and assisted living facilities in Maryland and Washington D.C. are copied at the end of this F-Tag section.

THE REGULATIONS

§483.10(i) Safe Environment.

The resident has a right to a safe, clean, comfortable and homelike environment, including but not limited to receiving treatment and supports for daily living safely.

The facility must provide—

§483.10(i)(1) A safe, clean, comfortable, and homelike environment, allowing the resident to use his or her personal belongings to the extent possible.

- **(i) This includes ensuring that the resident can receive care and services safely and that the physical layout of the facility maximizes resident independence and does not pose a safety risk The facility shall exercise reasonable care for the protection of the resident's property from loss or theft.**

§483.10(i)(2) Housekeeping and maintenance services necessary to maintain a sanitary, orderly, and comfortable interior;

§483.10(i)(3) Clean bed and bath linens that are in good condition;

§483.10(i)(4) Private closet space in each resident room, as specified in §483.90 (e)(2)(iv);

§483.10(i)(5) Adequate and comfortable lighting levels in all areas;

§483.10(i)(6) Comfortable and safe temperature levels. Facilities initially certified after October 1, 1990 must maintain a temperature range of 71 to 81°F; and

§483.10(i)(7) For the maintenance of comfortable sound levels.

DEFINITIONS §483.10(i)

"Adequate lighting"

means levels of illumination suitable to tasks the resident chooses to perform or the facility staff must perform. **(For the mandated illumination levels in Maryland and the District of Columbia, see the full Voices for Quality Care Handbook)**

"Comfortable lighting"

means lighting that minimizes glare and provides maximum resident control, where feasible, over the intensity, location, and direction **of lighting to meet their needs** or enhance independent functioning.

"Comfortable and safe temperature levels"

means that the ambient temperature *should* be in a relatively narrow range that minimizes residents' susceptibility to loss of body heat and risk of hypothermia, *or hyperthermia*, or and is *comfortable for the residents.*

"Comfortable sound levels"

do not interfere with resident's hearing and enhance privacy when privacy is desired, and encourage interaction when social participation is desired. Of particular concern to comfortable sound levels is the resident's control over unwanted noise.

"Environment"

refers to any environment in the facility that is frequented by residents, including (but not limited to) the residents' rooms, bathrooms, hallways, dining areas, lobby, outdoor patios, therapy areas and activity areas.

A "homelike environment"

is one that de-emphasizes the institutional character of the setting, to the extent possible, and allows the resident to use those personal belongings that support a homelike environment. A determination of "homelike" **should** *include the resident's opinion of the living environment.*

"Orderly"

is defined as an uncluttered physical environment that is neat and well-kept

"Sanitary"

includes, but is not limited to, preventing the spread of disease-causing organisms by keeping resident care equipment clean and properly stored. Resident care equipment includes, **but is not limited to, equipment used in the completion of the activities of daily living.**

GUIDANCE: EXERPTS FROM THE SURVEYOR'S GUIDELINES §483.10(i)

A personalized, homelike environment recognizes the individuality and autonomy of the resident, provides an opportunity for self-expression, and encourages links with the past and family members. The intent of the word "homelike" in this regulation is that the nursing home should provide an environment as close to that of the environment of a private home as possible.

This concept of creating a home setting includes the elimination of institutional odors, and practices to the extent possible. ***Some practices that can be eliminated to decrease the institutional character of the environment include, but are not limited to, the following:***

- Overhead paging *(including frequent announcements)* and piped-in music throughout the building.
- Meal service using trays (some residents may wish to eat certain meals on trays).

- Institutional signs labeling work rooms/closets in areas visible to residents and the public.
- Medication *or treatment* carts (some innovative facilities store medications in locked areas in resident rooms *or in secured carts that appear like furniture)*.
- The widespread and long-term use of audible chair and bed alarms, instead of their limited use for selected residents for diagnostic purposes or according to their care planned needs. These devices can startle the resident and constrain the resident from normal repositioning movements, which can be problematic.
- Furniture *that does not reflect a home-like environment or is uncomfortable; the absence of window treatments or drapes; the lack of textures or the absence of bedspreads or personal items in rooms or on walls.*
- Large, centrally located nursing/care team stations, *including those with barriers (such as Plexiglas) that prevent the staff from interacting with residents.*

Many facilities cannot immediately make these types of changes, but it should be a goal for all facilities that have not yet made these types of changes to work toward them.

A "homelike" environment is not achieved simply through enhancements to the physical environment. It concerns striving for person-centered care that emphasizes individualization, relationships and a psychosocial environment that welcomes each resident and makes her/him comfortable. *It is the responsibility of all facility staff to create a "homelike" environment and promptly address any cleaning needs.*

In a facility in which most *residents* come for a short-term stay, residents would not typically move his or her bedroom furniture into the room, but may desire to bring a television, chair or other personal belongings to have while staying in the facility. *There needs to be sufficient individual closet space so that resident clothing is kept separate from a roommate's. Closets must be structured so the resident can get to and reach their hanging clothing whenever they choose. Out-of-season items may be stored in alternate locations outside the resident's room.*

Adequate lighting design has these features:

- Lighting with minimum glare in areas frequented by residents. Elimination of high levels of glare produced by shiny flooring and from unshielded window openings;
- Even light levels in common areas and hallways, avoiding patches of low light caused by too much space between light fixtures, within limits of building design constraints;
- Use of daylight as much as possible;
- Extra lighting, such as table and floor lamps to provide sufficient light to assist residents with tasks such as reading;
- Lighting for residents who need to find their way from bed to bathroom at night (*for example*, red colored night lights preserve night vision); and
- Dimming switches in resident rooms (where possible and when desired by the resident) so that staff can tend to a resident at night with limited disturbances to them or a roommate. If dimming is not feasible, another option may be for staff to use flashlights/pen lights when they provide night care.

While facilities certified after October 1, 1990, *are required to maintain an air temperature range of 71-81°F, there may be brief periods of time where* that temperature *falls outside of that range* only during rare, *brief periods of unseasonable weather*. This interpretation would apply in cases where it does not adversely affect resident health and safety, *and facility staff took appropriate steps to ensure resident comfort. This* would enable facilities in areas of the country with relatively cold or hot climates to avoid the expense of installing equipment that would only be needed infrequently.

Lighting in Maryland Nursing Homes

COMAR 10.07.02.26 (I—K) —Nursing Home Regulations
(Maryland)(formatting altered by Voices)

I. Lighting—New Construction and Existing Facilities. Each patient's
room shall be lighted by outside windows and also shall have artificial
light adequate for reading and other uses as required. All entrances,
hallways, stairways, inclines, ramps, basements, attics, storerooms,
kitchens, laundries, and service units shall have sufficient artificial
lighting to prevent accidents and promote efficiency of service

J. Minimally Maintained Lighting Levels—New Construction and
Existing Facilities. Lighting shall be adequate for activities conducted in
given area

Area Minimum Lighting

(1) Administrative areas— 30 foot candles

(2) Dining areas— 30 foot candles

(3) Recreation areas—100 foot candles

(4) Patient's room— 10 foot candles

(5) Patient's reading lamps— 30 foot candles

(6) Nurses' station—20 foot candles

(7) Medicine storage and preparation area—100 foot candles

(8) Stairways—20 foot candles

(9) Corridors—20 foot candles

Night Lights—New Construction and Existing Facilities. There shall be
sufficient lighting at night in selected areas of the facility (hallways,

stairs and designated toilets) for the safety of the patient who must get up during the night. There also shall be one night light in each bedroom for patients. In new construction the night light shall be switched at the patient room door.

Lighting in Maryland Assisted Living Facilities

COMAR 10.07.14.51—Assisted Living Facilities (Maryland)

.51 Illumination.

A. Resident's Room.

- *(1) An assisted living program shall ensure that a resident's room:*
  - *(a) Is lighted by an outside window that:*
    - *(i) Contains a glass surface; and*
    - *(ii) Has square footage at least equal to 10 percent of the room's required floor area;*
  - *(b) Has a minimum of 60 wattage or the equivalent of artificial light provided for reading; and*
  - *(c) Is provided with additional artificial light as required for other uses, such as night lights to enable residents to get to the bathroom at night.*
- *(2) An assisted living program shall provide additional lighting or wattage upon reasonable request by the resident or the resident's legal representative.*

B. Common Use Areas. An assisted living program shall ensure that common use areas, such as entrances, hallways, inclines, ramps, cellars, attics, storerooms, kitchens, and laundries, have sufficient artificial lighting to prevent accidents and promote efficient service.

C. The assisted living program shall provide sufficient light to meet the resident's needs.

District of Columbia Regulations (regarding lighting in nursing homes and assisted living facilities as of 4/7/2015

Lighting in DC Nursing Homes

3234.10The following minimum lighting levels shall be used throughout the facility:

MINIMUM LIGHTING LEVELS (FOOT–CANDLES ON THE TASK)

Barber/Beauty area 50 foot candles

Corridors 20

Nursing areas (day) 10

Nursing areas (night) 50

Dietary 15

Elevators 50

Examination room 50

Employee Lounge 20

Employee Locker Room 30

Linens 30

Sorting soiled linens 10

Central (clean) linen supply 15

Linens rooms/closets 20

Janitor closet 30

Lobby 50

General 50

Receptionist 50

Administrative spaces 30

General office 30

Medical records 50

Conference/interview area/room 50

Mechanical/electrical room/space 50

Nursing station 20

   General 10

   Desk 30

   Medication area 50

   Nourishment center 15

Corridors (day) 30

Corridors (night) 30

Occupational therapy 30

   Work area, general 15

   Work benches/tables 30

Resident room 30

   General 30

   Reading/bed 15

   Toilet 20

Physical Therapy 30

Resident Lounge

   General 15

   Reading 30

Resident dining 30

Speech therapy 30

Stairways 15

Storage, general 20

Toilet/shower/bath 30

3234.10 Every habitable room shall contain windows of size, area, and specifications in accordance with the 1996 BOCA National Building Code.

3234.11 In habitable rooms, windows shall be of openable type, with sills no higher than three (3) feet above the floor.

SOURCE: Notice of Final Rulemaking published at 49 DCR 473 (January 18, 2002).

Lighting in Assisted Living Facilities

DC ST § 44-110.07
Chapter 1. Assisted Living Residence Regulation. Subchapter X. Facility Regulations.

§ 44-110.07. Health, light, and ventilation.

(a) An ALR shall ensure that each facility is lighted and ventilated in accordance with Title 12 of the District of Columbia Municipal Regulations (District of Columbia Construction Codes Supplement of 1992). Artificial night lights for corridors and exterior security lighting shall be installed.

(b) Each room shall have either a functioning ceiling light fixture or another source of artificial light.

F585—Grievances

THE REGULATIONS

§483.10(j) Grievances.

§483.10(j)(1) The resident has the right to voice grievances *to the facility or other agency or entity that hears grievances* without discrimination or reprisal *and without fear of discrimination or reprisal*. Such grievances include those with respect to care and treatment which has been furnished as well as that which has not been furnished, *the behavior of staff and of other residents, and other concerns regarding their LTC facility stay.*

§483.10(j)(2) The resident has the right to *and the facility must make prompt efforts by the facility to resolve grievances the resident may have, in accordance with this paragraph*

§483.10(j)(3) The facility must make information on how to file a grievance or complaint available to the resident.

§483.10(j)(4) The facility must establish a grievance policy to ensure the prompt resolution of all grievances regarding the residents' rights contained in this paragraph. Upon request, the provider must give a copy of the grievance policy to the resident. The grievance policy must include:

- *(i) Notifying resident individually or through postings in prominent locations throughout the facility of the right to file grievances orally (meaning spoken) or in writing; the right to file grievances anonymously; the contact information of the grievance official with whom a grievance can be filed, that is, his or her name, business address (mailing and email) and business phone number; a reasonable expected time frame for completing the review of the grievance; the right to obtain a written decision regarding his or her grievance; and the contact information of independent entities with whom grievances may be filed, that is, the pertinent State agency, Quality Improvement Organization, State Survey Agency and State Long-Term Care Ombudsman program or protection and advocacy system;*

- *(ii) Identifying a Grievance Official who is responsible for overseeing the grievance process, receiving and tracking grievances through to their conclusions; leading any necessary investigations by the facility; maintaining the confidentiality of all information associated with grievances, for example, the identity of the resident for those grievances submitted anonymously, issuing written grievance decisions to the resident; and coordinating with state and federal agencies as necessary in light of specific allegations;*

- *(iii) As necessary, taking immediate action to prevent further potential violations of any resident right while the alleged violation is being investigated;*

- *(iv) Consistent with §483.12(c)(1), immediately reporting all alleged violations involving neglect, abuse, including injuries of unknown source, and/or misappropriation of resident property, by anyone furnishing services on behalf of the provider, to the administrator of the provider; and as required by State law;*

- *(v) Ensuring that all written grievance decisions include the date the grievance was received, a summary statement of the resident's grievance, the steps taken to investigate the grievance, a summary of the pertinent findings or conclusions regarding the resident's concerns(s), a statement as to whether the grievance was confirmed or not confirmed, any corrective action taken or to be taken by the facility as a result of the grievance, and the date the written decision was issued;*

- *(vi) Taking appropriate corrective action in accordance with State law if the alleged violation of the residents' rights is confirmed by the facility or if an outside entity*

having jurisdiction, such as the State Survey Agency,
Quality Improvement Organization, or local law
enforcement agency confirms a violation for any of these
residents' rights within its area of responsibility; and

Maintaining evidence demonstrating the result of all
grievances for a period of no less than 3 years from the
issuance of the grievance decision.

DEFINITIONS §483.10(j)

"Prompt efforts to resolve"

include facility acknowledgment of a complaint/grievance and actively
working toward resolution of that complaint/grievance.

#

F586—Resident Contact with External Entities

THE REGULATIONS

§483.10(k) Contact with External Entities.

A facility must not prohibit or in any way discourage a resident from communicating with federal, state, or local officials, including, but not limited to, federal and state surveyors, other federal or state health department employees, including representatives of the Office of the State Long-Term Care Ombudsman and any representative of the agency responsible for the protection and advocacy system for individuals with mental disorder (established under the Protection and Advocacy for Mentally Ill Individuals Act of 2000 (42 U.S.C. 10801 et seq.), regarding any matter, whether or not subject to arbitration or any other type of judicial or regulatory action.

INTENT §483.10(k)

Facility staff must ensure that residents are able to communicate freely with representatives of these entities for whatever matter.

#

483.12 Freedom from Abuse, Neglect, and Exploitation

F600—*Free from Abuse and Neglect

FOR VOICES FOR QUALITY CARE ADVOCATES

In cases where abuse or neglect is suspected, consult the Surveyor's Guidelines. There is a very large detailed section under F-600 with far too much information to include in this manual.

> https://www.cms.gov/Medicare/Provider-Enrollment-and-Certification/GuidanceforLawsAndRegulations/Downloads/Advance-Appendix-PP-Including-Phase-2-.pdf

THE REGULATIONS

§483.12 Freedom from Abuse, Neglect, and Exploitation

The resident has the right to be free from abuse, **neglect, misappropriation of resident property, and exploitation as defined in this subpart. This includes but is not limited to freedom** from corporal punishment, involuntary seclusion **and any physical or chemical restraint not required to treat the resident's medical symptoms**

§483.12(a) The facility must—

§483.12(a)(1) Not use verbal, mental, sexual, or physical abuse, corporal punishment, or involuntary seclusion;

DEFINITIONS

"Abuse,"

is defined at §483.5 as "the willful infliction of injury, unreasonable confinement, intimidation, or punishment with resulting physical harm, pain or mental anguish. *Abuse* also includes the deprivation by an individual, including a caretaker, of goods or services that are necessary to attain or maintain physical, mental, and psychosocial well-being. *Instances of abuse of all residents, irrespective of any mental or physical condition, cause physical harm, pain or mental anguish. It includes verbal abuse, sexual abuse, physical abuse, and mental abuse including abuse facilitated or enabled through the use of technology."*

"Neglect,"

as defined at §483.5, means "the failure *of the facility, its employees or service providers* to provide goods and services *to a resident that are* necessary to avoid physical harm, *pain*, mental *anguish or emotional distress."*

"Sexual abuse,"

is defined at §483.5 as "non-consensual sexual contact of any type with a resident."

"Willful,"

as defined at §483.5 and as used in the definition of "abuse," "means the individual must have acted deliberately, not that the individual must have intended to inflict injury or harm."

#

F602— Free from Misappropriation/Exploitation

FOR VOICES FOR QUALITY CARE ADVOCATES

This regulation is helpful in situations Voices Advocates have often encountered where staff, in order to clothe a resident lacking in certain clothing items, without permission "borrows" clothing from another resident either in the laundry or from the closet of the other resident.

An Advocate with a case that may involve misappropriation or exploitation should consult the Surveyor's Guidelines for additional information on this issue.

THE REGULATIONS

§483.12

The resident has the right to be free from abuse, **neglect, misappropriation of resident property, and exploitation as defined in this subpart. This includes but is not limited to freedom** from corporal punishment, involuntary seclusion **and any physical or chemical restraint not required to treat the resident's medical symptoms**

DEFINITIONS

"Exploitation,"

as defined at §483.5, means "taking advantage of a resident for personal gain, through the use of manipulation, intimidation, threats, or coercion."

"Misappropriation of resident property,"

as defined at §483.5, means "the deliberate misplacement, exploitation, or wrongful, temporary, or permanent use of a resident's belongings or money without the resident's consent."

GUIDANCE: EXERPTS FROM THE SURVEYOR'S GUIDELINES

Residents' property includes all residents' possessions, regardless of their apparent value to others since they may hold intrinsic value to the resident. Residents are permitted to keep personal clothing and possessions for their use while in the facility, as long as it does not infringe upon the rights of other residents (See F557). Examples of resident property include jewelry, clothing, furniture, money, and electronic devices, the resident's personal information such as name and identifying information, credit cards, bank accounts, driver's licenses, and social security cards.

Examples of misappropriation of resident property include, but are not limited to:

- *Identity theft;*
- *Theft of money from bank accounts;*
- *Unauthorized or coerced purchases on a resident's credit card;*
- *Unauthorized or coerced purchases from resident's funds;*
- *A resident who provides a gift to staff in order to receive ongoing care, based on staff's persuasion; and*
- *A resident who provides monetary assistance to staff, after staff had made the resident believe that staff was in a financial crisis.*

Facility staff are in a position that may be perceived as one of power over a resident. As such, staff may be able to manipulate or unduly influence decisions by the resident. Staff must not accept or ask a resident to borrow personal items or money, nor should they attempt to gain access to a resident's holdings, money, or personal possessions through persuasion, coercion, request for a loan, or solicitation. For example, exploitation may include, but is not limited to, when a resident, or resident representative, has given his/her money or belongings to staff as a result of coercion, or because the resident, or resident representative, believes that it was necessary (e.g., in order to receive good care). A resident's apparent consent is not valid if it is obtained from a resident lacking the capacity to consent, or consent is obtained through intimidation, coercion or fear, whether it is expressed by the resident or suspected by staff.

Another example of misappropriation of resident property is the diversion of a resident's medication(s), including, but not limited to, controlled substances for staff use or personal gain.

F603— Free from Involuntary Seclusion

FOR VOICES FOR QUALITY CARE ADVOCATES

Consult this section also for people living in locked units. Voices Advocates have had cases where family members have incorrectly placed people in locked units. Always check for valid POA or Guardianship documents.

THE REGULATIONS

§483.12

The resident has the right to be free from abuse, **neglect, misappropriation of resident property, and exploitation as defined in this subpart. This includes but is not limited to freedom** from corporal punishment, involuntary seclusion **and any physical or chemical restraint not required to treat the resident's medical symptoms.**

§483.12(a) The facility must—

§483.12(a)(1) Not use verbal, mental, sexual, or physical abuse, corporal punishment, or involuntary seclusion;

DEFINITIONS

"Involuntary seclusion"

*is defined as separation of a resident from other residents or from her/his room or confinement to her/his room (with or without roommates) against the resident's will, or the will of the **resident** representative.*

GUIDANCE: EXERPTS FROM THE SURVEYOR'S GUIDELINES

Involuntary seclusion may take many forms, including but not limited to the confinement, restriction or isolation of a resident. Involuntary seclusion may be a result of staff convenience, a display of power from the caregiver over the resident, or may be used to discipline a resident for wandering, yelling, repeatedly requesting care or services, using the call light, disrupting a program or activity, or refusing to allow care or services such as showering or bathing to occur.

Involuntary seclusion includes, but is not limited to, the following:

- *A resident displays disruptive behaviors, such as yelling, screaming, distracting others (such as standing and obstructing others viewing abilities for the TV or programs) and staff remove and seclude the resident in a separate location such as in an office area or his/her room, leaving and closing the door and without providing interventions to address the behavioral symptoms;*
- *In an attempt to isolate a resident in order to prevent him/her from leaving an area, the resident(s) is involuntarily confined to an area by staff placing furniture, carts, chairs in front of doorways or areas of egress;*
- *Staff hold a door shut, from the opposite side of the door, in order to prevent egress;*
- *Staff place a resident in a darkened room, office, or area secluded from other staff and residents for convenience or as punishment;*
- *A resident is physically placed in an area without access to call lights, and/or other methods of communication*

120

creating an environment of seclusion and isolation for the resident; and

- *A resident placed in a secured area of the facility, but does not meet the criteria for the unit and is not provided with access codes or other information for independent egress.*

Considerations Involving Secured/Locked Areas

If a resident resides in a secured/locked area that restricts a resident's movement throughout the facility, the facility must ensure that the resident is free from involuntary seclusion.

A resident in a secured/locked area would not be considered to be involuntarily secluded if all of the following are met:

- *The facility has identified the clinical criteria for placing a resident in the secured/locked area;*
- *Placement in a secured/locked area is not*
  - *(1) Used for staff convenience or discipline;*
  - *(2) Based on the resident's diagnosis alone since the determination for placement in the area must be made on an individualized basis; and/or*
  - *(3) Based on a request from the resident's representative or family member without clinical justification;*

For example, if the POA requests placement in the secured/locked area but the resident declines placement and placement does not meet the clinical criteria and is not in the best interest of the resident, then placement of the resident in the secured/locked area would be involuntary seclusion.

- *The facility involves the resident/representative in care planning, including the decision for placement in a secured/locked area and the development of interventions based upon the resident's comprehensive assessment and needs; and*

- *The facility provides immediate access and visitation by family, resident representative or other individuals, subject to reasonable clinical and safety restrictions and the resident's right to deny or withdraw consent.*

NOTE: A resident who chooses to live in the secured/locked unit (e.g., the spouse of a resident who resides in the area), and does not meet the criteria for placement, must have access to the method of opening doors independently. The chosen method for opening doors (e.g., distribution of access code information) is not specified by CMS. Staff should be aware of which residents have access to opening doors and monitor their use of the access to ensure other residents' safety.

F604— Right to be Free from Physical Restraints

THE REGULATIONS

§483.10(e) Respect and Dignity.

The resident has a right to be treated with respect and dignity, including:

§483.10(e)(1) The right to be free from any physical or chemical restraints imposed for purposes of discipline or convenience, and not required to treat the resident's medical symptoms, *consistent with §483.12(a)(2).*

§483.12

The resident has the right to be free from abuse, *neglect, misappropriation of resident property, and exploitation as defined in this subpart. This includes but is not limited to freedom* from corporal punishment, involuntary seclusion *and any physical or chemical restraint not required to treat the resident's medical symptoms*

§483.12(a) The facility must—

§483.12(a)(2) Ensure that the resident is free from physical or chemical restraints imposed for purposes of discipline or convenience and that are not required to treat the resident's medical symptoms. When the use of restraints is indicated, the facility must use the least restrictive alternative for the least amount of time and document ongoing re-evaluation of the need for restraints.

INTENT

The intent of this requirement is for each resident to attain and maintain his/her highest practicable well-being in an environment that:

- Prohibits the use of physical restraints for discipline or convenience;
- **Prohibits the use of physical restraints to unnecessarily inhibit a resident's freedom of movement or activity; and**
- Limits **physical** restraint use to circumstances in which the resident has medical symptoms that **may** warrant the use of restraints.

When a physical restraint is used, the facility must:

- **Use the least restrictive restraint for the least amount of time; and**
- **Provide ongoing re-evaluation of the need for the physical restraint.**

DEFINITIONS

"Convenience"

is defined as **the result of any *action that has the effect of altering* a** resident's behavior *such that the resident requires* a lesser amount of effort *or care*, and *is* not in the resident's best interest.

"Discipline"

is defined as any action taken by the facility for the purpose of punishing or penalizing residents.

"Freedom of movement"

means any change in place or position for the body or any part of the body that the person is physically able to control.

"Manual method"

means to hold or limit a resident's voluntary movement by using body contact as a method of physical restraint.

"Medical symptom"

is defined as an indication or characteristic of a physical or psychological condition.

"Position change alarms"

are alerting devices intended to monitor a resident's movement. The devices emit an audible signal when the resident moves in certain ways.

"Physical restraint"

is defined as any manual method, physical or mechanical device, *equipment, or* material that *meets all of the following criteria:*

- Is attached or adjacent to the resident's body;

- Cannot be removed easily *by the resident; and*

- Restricts *the resident's* freedom of movement or normal access to *his/her* body.

"Removes easily"

means that the manual method, *physical or mechanical* device, equipment, or material, can be removed intentionally by the resident in the same manner as it was applied by the staff.

GUIDANCE: EXERPTS FROM THE SURVEYOR'S GUIDELINES

Examples of facility practices that meet the definition of a *physical* restraint include, but are not limited to:

- Using *bed* rails that keep a resident from voluntarily getting out of bed;

- Placing a chair or bed close **enough** to a wall that the **resident is prevented** from rising out of the chair or voluntarily getting out of bed;
- *Placing a resident on a concave mattress so that the resident cannot independently get out of bed;*
- Tucking in **a sheet tightly so that the resident cannot get out of bed,** or fastening fabric or clothing so that a resident's **freedom of movement** is restricted;
- Placing a resident in a chair, **such as a beanbag or recliner**, that prevents a resident from rising **independently;**
- Using devices in conjunction with a chair, such as trays, tables, **cushions**, bars or belts, that the resident cannot remove and prevents the resident from rising;
- *Applying leg or arm restraints, hand mitts, soft ties or vests that the resident cannot remove;*
- *Holding down a resident in response to a behavioral symptom or during the provision of care if the resident is resistive or refusing the care;*
- *Placing a resident in an enclosed framed wheeled walker, in which the resident cannot open the front gate or if the device has been altered to prevent the resident from exiting the device; and*
- *Using a position change alarm to monitor resident movement, and the resident is afraid to move to avoid setting off the alarm.*

F605— Right to be Free from Chemical Restraints

THE REGULATIONS

§483.10(e) Respect and Dignity.

The resident has a right to be treated with respect and dignity, including:

§483.10(e)(1) The right to be free from any physical or chemical restraints imposed for purposes of discipline or convenience, and not required to treat the resident's medical symptoms, *consistent with §483.12(a)(2).*

§483.12

The resident has the right to be free from abuse, *neglect, misappropriation of resident property, and exploitation as defined in this subpart. This includes but is not limited to freedom* from corporal punishment, involuntary seclusion *and any physical or chemical restraint not required to treat the resident's medical symptoms.*

§483.12(a) The facility must—

§483.12(a)(2) Ensure that the resident is free from physical or chemical restraints imposed for purposes of discipline or convenience and that are not required to treat the resident's medical symptoms. When the use of restraints is indicated, the facility must use the least restrictive alternative for the least amount of time and document ongoing re-evaluation of the need for restraints.

DEFINITIONS

"Chemical restraint"

is defined as any drug that is used for discipline or staff convenience and not required to treat medical symptoms.

"Convenience"

is defined as *the result of* any *action that has the effect of altering* a resident's behavior *such that the resident requires* a lesser amount of effort *or care*, and *is* not in the resident's best interest.

"Discipline"

is defined as any action taken by facility staff for the purpose of punishing or penalizing residents.

"Indication for use"

is defined as the identified, documented clinical rationale for administering a medication that is based upon an assessment of the resident's condition and therapeutic goals and is consistent with manufacturer's recommendations and/or clinical practice guidelines, clinical standards of practice, medication references, clinical studies or evidence-based review articles that are published in medical and/or pharmacy journals.

"Medical symptom"

is defined as an indication or characteristic of a medical, physical or psychological condition.

GUIDANCE: EXERPTS FROM THE SURVEYOR'S GUIDELINES

Determination of Indication for Medication Use

The clinical record must reflect the following:

- *Whether there is an adequate indication for use for the medication (e.g., a psychotropic medication is not administered unless the medication is used to treat a specific condition);*

- *Whether an excessive dose and/or duration of the medication was administered to the resident;*
- *Whether there is adequate monitoring for the effectiveness of the medication in treating the specific condition and for any adverse consequences resulting from the medication;*
- *Whether a resident who uses a psychotropic drug(s) is receiving gradual dose reduction and behavioral interventions, unless clinically contraindicated; and*
- *Whether a resident who receives a psychotropic drug(s) pursuant to a PRN (pro re nata, or as needed) order is not administered the medication unless the medication is necessary to treat a diagnosed specific symptom, as documented in the clinical record.*

#

F606— Not Employ/Engage Staff with Adverse Actions

FOR VOICES FOR QUALITY CARE ADVOCATES

A surprising number of nursing homes have been cited for hiring staff with a history of abuse or neglect. A Voices Volunteer encountering a helpline caller complaint involving a possible violation of this F-Tag should check all past survey reports on either the CMS Nursing Home Compare website or the ProPublica website for any relevant citations of deficiency.

THE REGULATIONS

§483.12(a) The facility must—

§483.12(a)(3) Not employ *or otherwise engage* individuals who—

- *(i)* Have been found guilty of *abuse, neglect, exploitation, misappropriation of property, or mistreatment* by a court of law;
- *(ii)* Have had a finding entered into the State nurse aide registry concerning abuse, neglect, *exploitation*, mistreatment of residents or misappropriation of their property; *or*
- *(iii) Have a disciplinary action in effect against his or her professional license by a state licensure body as a result of a finding of abuse, neglect, exploitation, mistreatment of residents or misappropriation of resident property.*

§483.12(a)(4) Report to the State nurse aide registry or licensing authorities any knowledge it has of actions by a court of law against an employee, which would indicate unfitness for service as a nurse aide or other facility staff.

INTENT

The facility must not hire an employee or engage an individual who was found guilty of abuse, neglect, exploitation, or mistreatment or misappropriation of property by a court of law; or who has a finding in the State nurse aide registry concerning abuse, neglect, exploitation, mistreatment of residents or misappropriation of resident property, or has had a disciplinary action in effect taken against his/her professional license. The facility must report knowledge of actions by a court of law against an employee that indicates the employee is unfit for duty.

DEFINITIONS

"Found guilty ... by a court of law"

applies to situations where the defendant pleads guilty, is found guilty, or pleads *no contest to charges of abuse, neglect, exploitation, misappropriation of property, or mistreatment*

"Finding"

is defined as a determination made by the State that validates allegations of abuse, neglect, *exploitation*, mistreatment of residents, or misappropriation of their property.

"Mistreatment,"

as defined at §483.5, means "inappropriate treatment or exploitation of a resident."

GUIDANCE: EXERPTS FROM THE SURVEYOR'S

Employment

NOTE: For purposes of this guidance, "staff" includes employees, the medical director, consultants, contractors, volunteers. Staff would also include caregivers who provide care and services to residents on behalf of the facility, students in the facility's nurse aide training program, and students from affiliated academic institutions, including therapy, social, and activity programs.

Facilities must be thorough in their investigations of the histories of prospective staff. In addition to inquiry of the State nurse aide registry or licensing authorities, the facility should check information from previous and/or current employers and make reasonable efforts to uncover information about any past criminal prosecutions. It has been reported that former nurse aides with a finding of abuse, neglect, misappropriation of resident property, exploitation, or mistreatment may seek employment in other departments of a facility, such as maintenance or laundry services/department, or at another nursing home in a non-nursing capacity.

F607— Develop/Implement Abuse/Neglect, etc. Policies

THE REGULATIONS

§483.12(b) The facility must develop and implement written policies and procedures that:

§483.12(b)(1) Prohibit **and prevent** abuse, neglect, **and exploitation** of residents and misappropriation of resident property,

§483.12(b)(2) Establish policies and procedures to investigate any such allegations, and

§483.12(b)(3) Include training as required at paragraph §483.95,

§483.12(b)(4) Establish coordination with the QAPI program required under §483.75. [§483.12(b)(4) will be implemented beginning November 28, 2019 (Phase 3)]

INTENT

This regulation was written to provide protections for the health, welfare and rights of each resident residing in the facility. In order to provide these protections, the facility must develop written policies and procedures to prohibit and prevent abuse, neglect, exploitation of residents, and misappropriation of resident property. These written policies must include, but are not limited to, the following components:

- *Screening;*
- *Training;*
- *Prevention;*
- *Identification;*
- *Investigation;*
- *Protection; and*

* *Reporting/response.*

In order to ensure that the facility is doing all that is within its control to prevent such occurrences, these policies must be implemented (i.e., carried out), otherwise, the policies and procedures would not be effective. The facility is expected to provide oversight and monitoring to ensure that its staff, who are agents of the facility, implement these policies during the provision of care and services to each resident residing in the facility. A facility cannot disown the acts of its staff, since the facility relies on them to meet the Medicare and Medicaid requirements for participation by providing care in a safe environment.

NOTE: For purposes of this guidance, "staff" includes employees, the medical director, consultants, contractors, volunteers. Staff would also include caregivers who provide care and services to residents on behalf of the facility, students in the facility's nurse aide training program, and students from affiliated academic institutions, including therapy, social, and activity programs.

###

F608—Reporting of Reasonable Suspicion of a Crime

THE REGULATIONS

§483.12(b) The facility must develop and implement written policies and procedures that:

§483.12(b)(5) Ensure reporting of crimes occurring in federally-funded long-term care facilities in accordance with section 1150B of the Act. The policies and procedures must include but are not limited to the following elements

- *(i) Annually notifying covered individuals, as defined at section 1150B(a)(3) of the Act, of that individual's obligation to comply with the following reporting requirements.*
  - *(A) Each covered individual shall report to the State Agency and one or more law enforcement entities for the political subdivision in which the facility is located any reasonable suspicion of a crime against any individual who is a resident of, or is receiving care from, the facility.*
  - *(B) Each covered individual shall report immediately, but not later than 2 hours after forming the suspicion, if the events that cause the suspicion result in serious bodily injury, or not later than 24 hours if the events that cause the suspicion do not result in serious bodily injury.*
- *(ii) Posting a conspicuous notice of employee rights, as defined at section 1150B(d)(3) of the Act.*
- *(iii) Prohibiting and preventing retaliation, as defined at section 1150B(d)(1) and (2) of the Act.*

INTENT

The intent is for the facility to develop and implement policies and procedures that:

- *Ensure reporting of crimes against a resident or individual receiving care from the facility occurring in nursing homes within prescribed timeframes to the appropriate entities, consistent with Section 1150B of the Act;*
- *Ensure that all covered individuals, such as the owner, operator, employee, manager, agent or contractor report reasonable suspicion of crimes, as required by Section 1150B of the Act;*
- *Provide annual notification for covered individuals of these reporting requirements;*
- *Post a conspicuous notice of employee rights, including the right to file a complaint; and*
- *Assure that any covered individual who makes a report to be made, or is in the process of making a report, is not retaliated against.*

DEFINITIONS

"Covered individual"

is anyone who is an owner, operator, employee, manager, agent or contractor of the facility (See section 1150B(a)(3) of the Act).

"Crime":

Section 1150B(b)(1) of the Act provides that a "crime" is defined by law of the applicable political subdivision where the facility is located. A political subdivision would be a city, county, township or village, or any local unit of government created by or pursuant to State law.

"Law enforcement,"

as defined in section 2011(13) of the Act, is the full range of potential responders to elder abuse, neglect, and exploitation including: police, sheriffs, detectives, public safety officers; corrections personnel; prosecutors; medical examiners; investigators; and coroners.

"Serious bodily injury"

means an injury involving extreme physical pain; involving substantial risk of death; involving protracted loss or impairment of the function of a bodily member, organ, or mental faculty; requiring medical intervention such as surgery, hospitalization, or physical

rehabilitation; or an injury resulting from criminal sexual abuse (See section 2011(19)(A) of the Act).

"Criminal sexual abuse":

In the case of "criminal sexual abuse" which is defined in section 2011(19)(B) of the Act (as added by section 6703(a)(1)(C) of the Affordable Care Act), serious bodily injury/harm shall be considered to have occurred if the conduct causing the injury is conduct described in section 2241 (relating to aggravated sexual abuse) or section 2242 (relating to sexual abuse) of Title 18, United States Code, or any similar offense under State law. In other words, serious bodily injury includes sexual intercourse with a resident by force or incapacitation or through threats of harm to the resident or others or any sexual act involving a child. Serious bodily injury also includes sexual intercourse with a resident who is incapable of declining to participate in the sexual act or lacks the ability to understand the nature of the sexual act.

GUIDANCE: EXERPTS FROM THE SURVEYOR'S GUIDELINES

NOTE: Once an individual suspects that a crime has been committed, facility staff must exercise caution when handling materials that may be used for evidence or for a criminal investigation. It has been reported that some investigations

137

were impeded due to washing linens or clothing, destroying documentation, bathing or cleaning the resident before the resident has been examined, or failure to transfer a resident to the emergency room for examination including obtaining a rape kit, if appropriate.

###

<u>F609— Reporting of Alleged Violations</u>

<u>THE REGULATIONS</u>

§483.12(c) In response to allegations of abuse, neglect, exploitation, or mistreatment, the facility must:

§483.12(c)(1) Ensure that all alleged violations involving abuse, neglect, *exploitation* or mistreatment, including injuries of unknown source and misappropriation of resident property, are reported immediately, *but not later than 2 hours after the allegation is made, if the events that cause the allegation involve abuse or result in serious bodily injury, or not later than 24 hours if the events that cause the allegation do not involve abuse and do not result in serious bodily injury*, to the administrator of the facility and to other officials (including to the State Survey *Agency and adult protective services where state law provides for jurisdiction in long-term care facilities*) in accordance with State law through established procedures.

§483.12(c)(4) Report the results of all investigations to the administrator or his or her designated representative and to other officials in accordance with State law, including to the State Survey *Agency*, within 5 working days of the incident, and if the alleged violation is verified appropriate corrective action must be taken.

<u>DEFINITIONS</u>

"Abuse,"

is defined at §483.5 as "the willful infliction of injury, unreasonable confinement, intimidation, or punishment with resulting physical harm, pain or mental anguish. Abuse also includes the deprivation by an individual, including a caretaker, of goods or services that are necessary to attain or maintain physical, mental, and psychosocial well-being. Instances of abuse of all residents, irrespective of any mental or physical condition, cause physical harm, pain or mental anguish. It includes verbal abuse, sexual abuse, physical abuse, and mental abuse including abuse facilitated or enabled through the use of technology."

"Alleged violation"

is a situation or occurrence that is observed or reported by staff, resident, relative, visitor or others but has not yet been investigated and, if verified, could be noncompliance with the Federal requirements related to mistreatment, exploitation, neglect, or abuse, including injuries of unknown source, and misappropriation of resident property.

"Exploitation,"

as defined at §483.5, means "taking advantage of a resident for personal gain, through the use of manipulation, intimidation, threats, or coercion."

"Immediately"

means as soon as possible, in the absence of a shorter State time frame requirement, but not later than 2 hours after the allegation is made, if the events that cause the allegation involve abuse or result in serious bodily injury, or not later than 24 hours if the events that cause the allegation do not involve abuse and do not result in serious bodily injury.

"Injuries of unknown source" –

An injury should be classified as an "injury of unknown source" when both of the following criteria are met:

The source of the injury was not observed by any person or the source of the injury could not be explained by the resident; and

The injury is suspicious because of the extent of the injury or the location of the injury (e.g., the injury is located in an area not generally vulnerable to trauma) or the number of injuries observed at one particular point in time or the incidence of injuries over time.

"Misappropriation of resident property,"

as defined at §483.5, means "the deliberate misplacement, exploitation, or wrongful, temporary, or permanent use of a resident's belongings or money without the resident's consent."

"Mistreatment,"

as defined at §483.5, is "inappropriate treatment or exploitation of a resident."

Neglect,"

as defined at §483.5, means "the failure of the facility, its employees or service providers to provide goods and services to a resident that are necessary to avoid physical harm, **pain**, mental **anguish or emotional distress."**

"Sexual abuse,"

is defined at §483.5 as "non-consensual sexual contact of any type with a resident."

GUIDANCE: EXERPTS FROM THE SURVEYOR'S GUIDELINES

REPORTING ALLEGED VIOLATIONS

It is the responsibility of the facility to ensure that all staff are aware of reporting requirements and to support an environment in which staff and others report all alleged violations of mistreatment, exploitation, neglect, or abuse, including injuries of unknown source, and misappropriation of resident property. Protection of residents can be compromised or impeded if individuals are fearful of reporting, especially if the alleged abuse has been carried out by a staff member. During investigations, some staff have stated that he/she was aware, or had knowledge, that the incident had occurred, but did not report because he/she did not think it met the definition of abuse, neglect, mistreatment, exploitation, or misappropriation of resident property. Anecdotal reports have indicated that failure to report an alleged violation may be due to, but not limited to, the following:

- *An individual's allegation is not believed due to a history of reporting false allegations;*
- *Staff fear of retaliation, or fear losing his/her job;*
- *Sympathy for co-workers, for example, not wanting to cause trouble for the co-worker;*
- *Communication, cultural, or language issues; or*
- *Residents/resident representatives may fear retaliation.*

F610— Investigate/Prevent/Correct Alleged Violation

THE REGULATIONS

§483.12(c) In response to allegations of abuse, neglect, exploitation, or mistreatment, the facility must:

§483.12(c)(2) Have evidence that all alleged violations are thoroughly investigated.

§483.12(c)(3) Prevent further potential abuse, *neglect, exploitation, or mistreatment* while the investigation is in progress.

§483.12(c)(4) Report the results of all investigations to the administrator or his or her designated representative and to other officials in accordance with State law, including to the State Survey *Agency*, within 5 working days of the incident, and if the alleged violation is verified appropriate corrective action must be taken.

###

483.15 Admission, transfer, and Discharge

F620— Admissions Policy

FOR VOICES FOR QUALITY CARE ADVOCATES

We occasionally encounter nursing homes that attempt to request or require family members to either pay for the first month or two for a resident or agree to pay the charges for nursing home care. The facility can require that care be paid for from the resident's funds only. No funds can be requested or required for care for any resident or potential resident who is eligible for Medicaid or Medicare funding. In other words, a family member never pays for anything unless that family member is voluntarily paying for services not covered by that insurance.

THE REGULATIONS

§483.15(a) Admissions policy.

§483.15(a)(1) The facility must establish and implement an admissions policy.

§483.15(a)(2) The facility must—

- (i) Not **request or** require residents or potential residents to waive their rights *as set forth in this subpart and in applicable state, federal or local licensing or certification laws, including but not limited to their rights* to Medicare or Medicaid; and
- (ii) Not *request or* require oral or written assurance that residents or potential residents are not eligible for, or will not apply for, Medicare or Medicaid benefits.
- *(iii) Not request or require residents or potential residents to waive potential facility liability for losses of personal property.*

144

§483.15(a)*(3)* The facility must not **request or** require a third party guarantee of payment to the facility as a condition of admission or expedited admission, or continued stay in the facility. However, the facility may **request and require a resident representative** who has legal access to a resident's income or resources available to pay for facility care to sign a contract, without incurring personal financial liability, to provide facility payment from the resident's income or resources.

§483.15(a)*(4)* In the case of a person eligible for Medicaid, a nursing facility must not charge, solicit, accept, or receive, in addition to any amount otherwise required to be paid under the State plan, any gift, money, donation, or other consideration as a precondition of admission, expedited admission or continued stay in the facility. However,—

- (i) A nursing facility may charge a resident who is eligible for Medicaid for items and services the resident has requested and received, and that are not specified in the State plan as included in the term "nursing facility services" so long as the facility gives proper notice of the availability and cost of these services to residents and does not condition the resident's admission or continued stay on the request for and receipt of such additional services; and
- (ii) A nursing facility may solicit, accept, or receive a charitable, religious, or philanthropic contribution from an organization or from a person unrelated to a Medicaid eligible resident or potential resident, but only to the extent that the contribution is not a condition of admission, expedited admission, or continued stay in the facility for a Medicaid eligible resident.

§483.15(a)(5) States or political subdivisions may apply stricter admissions standards under State or local laws than are specified in this section, to prohibit discrimination against individuals entitled to Medicaid.

§483.15(a)*(6) A nursing facility must disclose and provide to a resident or potential resident prior to time of admission, notice of special characteristics or service limitations of the facility.*

§483.15(a)(7) A nursing facility that is a composite distinct part as defined in § 483.5 must disclose in its admission agreement its physical configuration, including the various locations that comprise the composite distinct part, and must specify the policies that apply to room changes between its different locations under paragraph (c)(9) of this section.

#

F621—Equal Practices Regardless of Payment Source

For information on these regulations see the Surveyor's Guidelines.

https://www.cms.gov/Medicare/Provider-Enrollment-and-Certification/GuidanceforLawsAndRegulations/Downloads/Advance-Appendix-PP-Including-Phase-2-.pdf

#

F622— Transfer and Discharge Requirement

FOR VOICES FOR QUALITY CARE ADVOCATES

This set of regulations is extremely important and is one that is often violated by certain nursing homes trying to achieve an involuntary discharge, trying to evict a resident against the resident's will for questionable reasons. Any Voices Advocate dealing with a discharge complaint of any kind must immediately consult the Voices Officers for guidance. In Maryland, these cases must be referred to the Long-Term Care Project at Legal Aid. The Advocate will need to initiate and monitor that contact. In Washington DC, the referral is to the attorney at the State Long-Term Care Ombudsman's Office. Legal assistance is necessary in any involuntary discharge case. This service is free to nursing home residents from both referral services listed in this paragraph.

There are only 6 valid reasons for discharging a person from a nursing home. Those reasons are listed in both sections below.

The first question to ask in an involuntary discharge case is, "do you have written notice of this discharge". If the answer is "no", the facility cannot proceed with the discharge. Facilities often orally inform a resident or a resident's representative

that the resident will need to transfer to another service when there is no valid reason for the discharge. In these cases, the facilities simply hope that the resident will actually move on this oral request knowing full well that they cannot actually discharge the resident under these circumstances. No paperwork, no discharge.

For additional information, see the Surveyor's Guidelines. For Maryland Regulations concerning notice of transfer within a nursing home, see the last section of this F-Tag.

THE REGULATIONS

§483.15(c) Transfer and discharge-

§483.15(c)(1) *Facility requirements-*

- *(i)* The facility must permit each resident to remain in the facility, and not transfer or discharge the resident from the facility unless—

The transfer or discharge is necessary for the resident's welfare and the resident's needs cannot be met in the facility;

- o *(A)* The transfer or discharge is appropriate because the resident's health has improved sufficiently so the resident no longer needs the services provided by the facility
- o *(B)* The safety of individuals in the facility is endangered *due* to the clinical or behavioral status of the resident;
- o *(C)* The health of individuals in the facility would otherwise be endangered;
- o *(D)* The resident has failed, after reasonable and appropriate notice, to pay for (or to have paid under Medicare or Medicaid) a stay at the facility. *Nonpayment applies if the resident does not submit the necessary paperwork for third party payment or after the third party, including Medicare or Medicaid,* denies the claim and the resident refuses to pay for his or her stay. For a resident who becomes eligible for Medicaid after admission to a *facility*, the facility may charge a resident only allowable charges under Medicaid; or

o (F) The facility ceases to operate.

- *(ii) The facility may not transfer or discharge the resident while the appeal is pending, pursuant to § 431.230 of this chapter, when a resident exercises his or her right to appeal a transfer or discharge notice from the facility pursuant to § 431.220(a)(3) of this chapter, unless the failure to discharge or transfer would endanger the health or safety of the resident or other individuals in the facility. The facility must document the danger that failure to transfer or discharge would pose.*

§483.15(c)(2) Documentation.

When the facility transfers or discharges a resident under any of the circumstances specified in paragraphs *(c)(1)(i)(A)* through *(F)* of this section, *the facility must ensure that the transfer or discharge is documented in* the resident's *medical* record *and appropriate information is communicated to the receiving health care institution or provider.*

- *(i) Documentation in the resident's medical record must include:*
  - o *(A) The basis for the transfer per paragraph (c)(1)(i) of this section.*
  - o *(B) In the case of paragraph (c)(1)(i)(A) of this section, the specific resident need(s) that cannot be met, facility attempts to meet the resident needs, and the service available at the receiving facility to meet the need(s).*
- *(ii)* The documentation *required by paragraph (c)(2)(i) of this section* must be made by—
  - o *(A)* The resident's physician when transfer or discharge is necessary under paragraph *(c) (1) (A)* or *(B)* of this section; and
  - o *(B)* A physician when transfer or discharge is necessary under paragraph *(c)(1)(i)(C) or (D)* of this section.
- *(iii) Information provided to the receiving provider must include a minimum of the following:*

o *(A) Contact information of the practitioner responsible for the care of the resident.*

o *(B) Resident representative information including contact information*

o *(C) Advance Directive information*

o *(D) All special instructions or precautions for ongoing care, as appropriate.*

o *(E) Comprehensive care plan goals;*

All other necessary information, including a copy of the resident's discharge summary, consistent with §483.21(c)(2) as applicable, and any other documentation, as applicable, to ensure a safe and effective transition of care.

GUIDANCE: EXERPTS FROM THE SURVEYOR'S GUIDELINES

In the following limited circumstances, facilities may initiate transfers or discharges:

- *1. The discharge or transfer is necessary for the resident's welfare and the facility cannot meet the resident's needs.*

- *2. The resident's health has improved sufficiently so that the resident no longer needs the care and/or services of the facility.*

- *3. The resident's clinical or behavioral status (or condition) endangers the safety of individuals in the facility.*

- *4. The resident's clinical or behavioral status (or condition) otherwise endangers the health of individuals in the facility.*

- *5. The resident has failed, after reasonable and appropriate notice to pay, or have paid under Medicare or Medicaid, for his or her stay at the facility.*

- *6. The facility ceases to operate.*

Transferring within a Facility in Maryland

In Maryland, when a facility intends to move a person to another room within the building, they must give the person at least 30 days notice of the intended move. This regulation applies only in the state of Maryland. For other states, if this is an issue, check the regulations for that state. **The following regulation comes from COMAR, Code of Maryland Regulations. This copy was made on May 22, 2014.**

10.07.09.12

.12 Resident Relocation and Bed Hold.

A. Notification of Resident Relocation Within a Facility.

(1) Except in emergency situations or when it is documented in the resident's record that a resident's physical, clinical, or psychological well being would be jeopardized, a nursing facility shall notify a resident or, when applicable, the resident's representative or interested family member, if available, in writing at least 30 days before the resident is relocated within a facility or to a different part of a facility, unless the resident or, if the resident is incapacitated, the resident's legally authorized representative, agrees to the relocation and this is documented in the resident's record.

(2) Under the limited conditions set forth in §A(1) of this regulation where 30 days notice cannot be provided in advance of a relocation, the facility shall document that it has provided notice of the relocation as soon as practicable.

(3) When a resident is relocated, the facility shall elicit and make reasonable efforts to comply with the resident's request of location and, if applicable, assignment of roommate.

###

F623— Notice Requirements Before Transfer/Discharge

FOR VOICES FOR QUALITY CARE ADVOCATES

This set of regulations is extremely important and is one that is often violated by certain nursing homes trying to achieve an involuntary discharge, trying to evict a resident against the resident's will for questionable reasons. Any Voices Advocate dealing with a discharge complaint of any kind must immediately consult the Voices Officers for guidance. In Maryland, these cases must be referred to the Long-Term Care Project at Legal Aid. The Advocate will need to initiate and monitor that contact. In Washington DC, the referral is to the attorney at the State Long-Term Care Ombudsman's Office. Legal assistance is necessary in any involuntary discharge case. This service is free to nursing home residents from both referral services listed in this paragraph.

There are only 6 valid reasons for discharging a person from a nursing home. Those reasons are listed in both sections below.

The first question to ask in an involuntary discharge case is, "do you have written notice of this discharge". If the answer is "no", the facility cannot proceed with the discharge. Facilities often orally inform a resident or a resident's representative that the resident will need to transfer to another service when there is no valid reason for the discharge. In these cases, the facilities simply hope that the resident will actually move on this oral request knowing full well that they cannot actually discharge the resident under these circumstances. No paperwork, no discharge.

For additional information, see the Surveyor's Guidelines. For Maryland Regulations concerning notice of transfer within a nursing home, see the last section of this F-Tag.

THE REGULATIONS

§483.15(c)(3) Notice before transfer.

Before a facility transfers or discharges a resident, the facility must—

Notify the resident and the **resident's** representative(s) of the transfer or discharge and the reasons for the move in writing and in a language and manner they understand. ***The facility must send a copy of the notice to a representative of the Office of the State Long-Term Care Ombudsman.***

- (i) Record the reasons *for the transfer or discharge* in the resident's **medical** record *in accordance with paragraph (c)(2) of this section;* and
- (ii) Include in the notice the items described in paragraph *(c)(5)* of this section.

§483.15(c)(4) Timing of the notice.

- (i) Except as specified in paragraphs *(c)(4)(ii) and (c)(8)* of this section, the notice of transfer or discharge required under this section must be made by the facility at least 30 days before the resident is transferred or discharged.
- (ii) Notice must be made as soon as practicable before transfer or discharge when—
  - (A) The safety of individuals in the facility would be endangered under paragraph *(c)(1)(i)(C)* of this section;
  - (B) The health of individuals in the facility would be endangered, under ***paragraph (c)(1)(i)(D)*** of this section;
  - (C) The resident's health improves sufficiently to allow a more immediate transfer or discharge, under paragraph *(c)(1)(i)(B)* of this section;
  - (D) An immediate transfer or discharge is required by the resident's urgent medical needs, under paragraph *(c)(1)(i)(A)* of this section; or
  - (E) A resident has not resided in the facility for 30 days.

§483.15(c)(5) Contents of the notice. The written notice specified in paragraph **(c)(3)** of this section must include the following:

- (i) The reason for transfer or discharge;
- (ii) The effective date of transfer or discharge;
- (iii) The location to which the resident is transferred or discharged;
- (iv) A statement of the resident's ***appeal rights, including the name, address (mailing and email), and telephone number of the entity which receives such requests; and information on how to obtain an appeal form and assistance in completing the form and submitting the appeal hearing request;***
- (v) The name, address (mailing and email) and telephone number of ***the Office of the*** State Long-Term Care Ombudsman;
- (vi) For nursing facility residents with ***intellectual and*** developmental disabilities ***or related disabilities***, the mailing ***and email*** address and telephone number of the agency responsible for the protection and advocacy of individuals ***with developmental disabilities*** established under Part C of the Developmental Disabilities Assistance and Bill of Rights Act ***of 2000 (Pub. L. 106-402, codified at 42 U.S.C. 15001 et seq.);*** and

For nursing facility residents ***with a*** mental ***disorder or related disabilities,*** the mailing ***and email*** address and telephone number of the agency responsible for the protection and advocacy of individuals ***with a mental disorder*** established under the Protection and Advocacy for Mentally Ill Individuals Act.

§483.15(c)(6) Changes to the notice.

If the information in the notice changes prior to effecting the transfer or discharge, the facility must update the recipients of the notice as soon as practicable once the updated information becomes available.

§483.15(c)(8) Notice in advance of facility closure

*In the case of facility closure, the individual who is the
administrator of the facility must provide written notification
prior to the impending closure to the State Survey Agency, the
Office of the State Long-Term Care Ombudsman, residents of
the facility, and the resident representatives, as well as the
plan for the transfer and adequate relocation of the residents,
as required at § 483.70(l).*

DEFINITIONS

"Facility-initiated transfer or discharge":

**A transfer or discharge which the resident objects to, did not originate
through a resident's verbal or written request, and/or is not in alignment
with the resident's stated goals for care and preferences.**

"Resident-initiated transfer or discharge":

**Means the resident or, if appropriate, the resident representative has
provided verbal or written notice of intent to leave the facility (leaving
the facility does not include the general expression of a desire to return
home or the elopement of residents with cognitive impairment).**

"Transfer and Discharge":

**Includes movement of a resident to a bed outside of the certified facility
whether that bed is in the same physical plant or not. Transfer and
discharge does not refer to movement of a resident to a bed within the
same certified facility. Specifically, transfer refers to the movement of a
resident from a bed in one certified facility to a bed in another certified
facility when the resident expects to return to the original facility.
Discharge refers to the movement of a resident from a bed in one
certified facility to a bed in another certified facility or other location in
the community, when return to the original facility is not expected.**

Transferring within a Facility in Maryland

In Maryland, when a facility intends to move a person to another room
within the building, they must give the person at least 30 days notice of

the intended move. This regulation applies only in the state of Maryland. For other states, if this is an issue, check the regulations for that state. **The following regulation comes from COMAR, Code of Maryland Regulations. This copy was made on May 22, 2014.**

10.07.09.12

.12 Resident Relocation and Bed Hold.

A. Notification of Resident Relocation Within a Facility.

(1) Except in emergency situations or when it is documented in the resident's record that a resident's physical, clinical, or psychological well being would be jeopardized, a nursing facility shall notify a resident or, when applicable, the resident's representative or interested family member, if available, in writing at least 30 days before the resident is relocated within a facility or to a different part of a facility, unless the resident or, if the resident is incapacitated, the resident's legally authorized representative, agrees to the relocation and this is documented in the resident's record.

(2) Under the limited conditions set forth in §A(1) of this regulation where 30 days notice cannot be provided in advance of a relocation, the facility shall document that it has provided notice of the relocation as soon as practicable.

(3) When a resident is relocated, the facility shall elicit and make reasonable efforts to comply with the resident's request of location and, if applicable, assignment of roommate.

F624— Preparation for Safe/Orderly Transfer/Discharge

§483.15(c)(7) Orientation for transfer or discharge.

A facility must provide and document sufficient preparation and orientation to residents to ensure safe and orderly transfer or discharge from the facility. ***This orientation must be provided in a form and manner that the resident can understand.***

#

F625— Notice of Bed Hold Policy Before/Upon Transfer

FOR VOICES FOR QUALITY CARE ADVOCATES

Maryland Medicaid no longer funds bed-holds for hospital admissions. In this state, only the federal regulations apply. In Washington DC, Medicaid pays for 18 days of bed-hold for hospital admissions.

THE REGULATIONS

§483.15(d) Notice of bed-hold policy and ***return—***

§483.15(d)(1) Notice before transfer. Before a nursing facility transfers a resident to a hospital or the resident ***goes*** on therapeutic leave, the nursing facility must provide written information to the ***resident or resident representative*** that specifies—

- (i) The duration of the ***state*** bed-hold policy, if any, during which the resident is permitted to return and resume residence in the nursing facility;
- (ii) ***The reserve bed payment policy in the state plan, under § 447.40 of this chapter, if any;***

- (iii)The nursing facility's policies regarding bed-hold periods, which must be consistent with paragraph *(e)(1)* of this section, permitting a resident to return; *and*

The information specified in paragraph (e)(1) of this section§483.15(d)(2) Bed-hold notice upon transfer. At the time of transfer of a resident for hospitalization or therapeutic leave, a nursing facility must provide to the resident and *the resident representative* written notice which specifies the duration of the bed-hold policy described in paragraph *(d)(1)* of this section.

INTENT

To ensure that residents are made aware of a facility's bed-hold and reserve bed payment policy before and upon transfer to a hospital or when taking a therapeutic leave of absence from the facility.

DEFINITIONS

"Bed-hold":

Holding or reserving a resident's bed while the resident is absent from the facility for therapeutic leave or hospitalization.

"Reserve Bed Payment":

Payments made by a State to the facility to hold a bed during a resident's temporary absence from a nursing facility.

"Therapeutic Leave":

Absences for purposes other than required hospitalization.

GUIDANCE

Notice of Bed-Hold Policy

All facilities must have policies that address holding a resident's bed during periods of absence, such as during hospitalization or therapeutic leave. Additionally, facilities must provide written information about these policies to residents prior to and upon transfer for such absences. This information must be provided to all facility residents, regardless of their payment source.

These **provisions** require **facilities to issue** two notices related to bed-hold policies. The first notice could be given well in advance of any transfer, **i.e., information provided in the admission packet.** Reissuance of the first notice would be required if the bed-hold policy under the State plan or the facility's policy were to change.

The second notice must be provided to the resident, and if applicable the resident's representative, at the time of transfer, or in cases of emergency transfer, within 24 hours. It is expected that facilities will document multiple attempts to reach the resident's representative in cases where the facility was unable to notify the representative.

The notice must provide information to the resident that explains the duration of bed-hold, if any, and the reserve bed payment policy. It should also address permitting the return of residents to the next available bed.

When a resident residing in a skilled nursing facility under Medicare is hospitalized or takes therapeutic leave, Medicare will not pay to hold the bed. Facility policies may allow the resident to pay privately to hold his or her bed. While the provisions of this requirement specifically address bed-hold under Medicaid law, facilities must make all residents aware in writing of their policies related to holding beds during absences from the facility NOTE: Residents not covered by Medicare or Medicaid, may be permitted to privately provide reserve bed payments.

Medicaid law requires each state Medicaid plan to address bed-hold policies for hospitalization and periods of therapeutic leave. State plans vary in payment for and duration of bed-holds. However, federal regulations do not require states to pay nursing facilities for holding beds while the resident is away from the facility. In general, the State plan sets the length of time, if any, that the state will pay the facility for holding a bed for a Medicaid-eligible resident. It is the responsibility of the survey team to know the bed-hold policies of their State Medicaid plan.

Additionally, §483.15 (e)(1) and F626 require facilities to permit residents to return to the facility immediately to the first available bed in a semi-private room.

The provision at §483.15(d)(1)(ii) references regulations for Medicaid Payments for Reserving Beds in Institutions (§447.40), which state "Absences for purposes other than required hospitalization (which cannot be anticipated and planned) are included in the patient's plan of care." This means that therapeutic leave of absence must be consistent with the resident's goals for care, be assessed by the comprehensive assessment, and incorporated into the comprehensive care plan, _and cannot be a means of involuntarily discharging the resident._

###

F626— Permitting Residents to Return to Facility

THE REGULATIONS

§483.15(e)(1) Permitting residents to return to facility.

A facility must establish and follow a written policy **on permitting residents to return to the facility after they are hospitalized or placed on therapeutic leave. The policy must provide for the following.**

- **(i)** A resident, whose hospitalization or therapeutic leave exceeds the bed-hold period under the State plan, **returns to the facility to their previous room if available or** immediately upon the first availability of a bed in a semi-private room if the resident—
    - (A) Requires the services provided by the facility; and
    - (B) Is eligible for **Medicare skilled nursing facility services or** Medicaid nursing facility services.
- **(ii) If the facility that determines that a resident who was transferred with an expectation of returning to the facility, cannot return to the facility, the facility must comply with the requirements of paragraph (c) as they apply to discharges.**

§483.15(e)(2) Readmission to a composite distinct part. When the facility to which a resident returns is a composite distinct part (as defined in § 483.5), the resident must be permitted to return to an available bed in the particular location of the composite distinct part in which he or she resided previously. If a bed is not available in that location at the time of return, the resident must be given the option to return to that location upon the first availability of a bed there.

INTENT

To ensure that facilities develop and implement policies that address bed-hold and return to the facility for all residents. Specifically, residents who are hospitalized or on therapeutic leave are allowed to return for skilled nursing or nursing facility care or services. In situations where the facility intends to discharge the resident, the facility must comply with Transfer and Discharge Requirements at §483.15(c), and the resident must be permitted to return and resume residence in the facility while an appeal is pending.

DEFINITIONS

"Bed-hold":

Holding or reserving a resident's bed while the resident is absent from the facility for therapeutic leave or hospitalization.

GUIDANCE §483.15 (e)

Facilities must develop *and implement* policies *for bed-hold and* permitting *residents to return following hospitalization or therapeutic leave. These policies must address how the facility will allow residents to return when their hospitalization or therapeutic leave has exceeded the bed-hold period allowed by the State Medicaid plan. Duration of and payment for bed-hold for residents eligible for Medicaid vary by State. The policy must also address how residents who pay privately, or receive Medicare, may pay to reserve their bed.*

NOTE: These requirements also apply to a resident who was receiving Medicaid at the time of his or her hospitalization, and returns needing skilled nursing (Medicare) care or services.

Residents must be permitted to return to their previous room, if available, or to the next available bed in a semi-private room, providing the resident:

- *Still requires the services provided by the facility; and*
- *Is eligible for Medicare skilled nursing facility or Medicaid nursing facility services.*

Medicaid-eligible residents must be **permitted to return** to the first available bed even if the residents have outstanding Medicaid balances.

<u>Not Permitting Residents to Return</u>

Not permitting a resident to return following hospitalization or therapeutic leave requires a facility to meet the requirements for a facility-initiated discharge as outlined in §483.15(c)(1)(ii). A facility must not discharge a resident unless:

- *1. The discharge or transfer is necessary for the resident's welfare and the facility cannot meet the resident's needs.*
- *2. The resident's health has improved sufficiently so that the resident no longer needs the services of the facility.*
- *3. The resident's clinical or behavioral status endangers the safety of individuals in the facility.*
- *4. The resident's clinical or behavioral status endangers the health of individuals in the facility.*
- *5. The resident has failed to pay for (or to have paid under Medicare or Medicaid) his or her stay at the facility.*
- *6. The facility ceases to operate.*

###

483.20 Resident Assessments

For the regulations in this category, see the Surveyor's Guidelines for the regulations and guidance sections.

https://www.cms.gov/Medicare/Provider-Enrollment-and-Certification/GuidanceforLawsAndRegulations/Downloads/Advance-Appendix-PP-Including-Phase-2-.pdf

The F-Tags under Resident Assessments are listed below.

F635—Admission Physician Orders for Immediate Care

F636—Comprehensive Assessments & Timing

F637—Comprehensive Assessment After Significant Change

F638—Quarterly Assessment At Least Every 3 Months

F639—Maintain 15 months of Resident Assessments

F640—Encoding/Transmitting Resident Assessment

F641—Accuracy of Assessments

F642—Coordination/Certification of Assessments

F644—Coordination of PASARR and Assessments

F645—PASARR Screening for MD and ID

F646—MD/ID Significant Change Notification

###

483.21 Comprehensive Resident Centered Care Plans

F655—Baseline Care Plan

FOR VOICES FOR QUALITY CARE ADVOCATES

The regulations under this F-Tag are included in the temporary moratorium on full enforcement.

THE REGULATIONS

§483.21 Comprehensive Person-Centered Care Planning

§483.21(a) Baseline Care Plans

§483.21(a)(1) The facility must develop and implement a baseline care plan for each resident that includes the instructions needed to provide effective and person-centered care of the resident that meet professional standards of quality care. The baseline care plan must—

- *(i) Be developed within 48 hours of a resident's admission.*
- *(ii) Include the minimum healthcare information necessary to properly care for a resident including, but not limited to—*
  - *(A)Initial goals based on admission orders.*
  - *(B) Physician orders.*
  - *(C) Dietary orders.*
  - *(D) Therapy services Social services.*
  - *(E) PASARR recommendation, if applicable.*

§483.21(a)(2) The facility may develop a comprehensive care plan in place of the baseline care plan if the comprehensive care plan—

- *(i) Is developed within 48 hours of the resident's admission.*
- *(ii) Meets the requirements set forth in paragraph (b) of this section (excepting paragraph (b)(2)(i) of this section).*

§483.21(a)(3) The facility must provide the resident and their representative with a summary of the baseline care plan that includes but is not limited to:

- *(i) The initial goals of the resident.*
- *(ii) A summary of the resident's medications and dietary instructions.*
- *(iii) Any services and treatments to be administered by the facility and personnel acting on behalf of the facility.*
- *(iv) Any updated information based on the details of the comprehensive care plan, as necessary.*

INTENT §483.21(a)

Completion and implementation of the baseline care plan within 48 hours of a resident's admission is intended to promote continuity of care and communication among nursing home staff, increase resident safety, and safeguard against adverse events that are most likely to occur right after admission; and to ensure the resident and representative, if applicable, are informed of the initial plan for delivery of care and services by receiving a written summary of the baseline care plan.

GUIDANCE: EXERPTS FROM THE SURVEYOR'S GUIDELINES

Person-centered care means the facility focuses on the resident as the center of control, and supports each resident in making his or her own choices. Person-centered care includes making an effort to understand what each resident is communicating, verbally and nonverbally, identifying what is important to each resident with regard to daily routines and preferred activities, and having an understanding of the resident's life before coming to reside in the nursing home.

The baseline care plan must reflect the resident's stated goals and objectives, and include interventions that address his or her current needs. It must be based on the admission orders, information about the resident available from the transferring provider, and discussion with the resident and resident representative, if applicable. Because the baseline care plan documents the interim approaches for meeting the resident's immediate needs, professional standards of quality care would dictate that it must also reflect changes to approaches, as necessary, resulting from significant changes in condition or needs, occurring prior to development of the comprehensive care plan. Facility staff must implement the interventions to assist the resident to achieve care plan goals and objectives.

###

F656—Develop/Implement Comprehensive Care Plan

FOR VOICES FOR QUALITY CARE ADVOCATES

In any Care Planning situation remember the resident has the right to be present and participate in a Care Planning Session. We very often find that residents are not included in Care Planning if they do not have a Representative who attends and insists that the Resident also attend. We have met many Residents who were totally unaware there were such things as Care Planning Conferences and were unaware of the items included in their own Care Plans.

Residents and their Representatives should have a copy of the care plan and should monitor it for compliance. Copies can be obtained cheaply if an electronic copy is requested.

THE REGULATIONS

§483.21(b) Comprehensive Care Plans

§483.21(b)(1) The facility must develop **and implement** a comprehensive **person-centered** care plan for each resident, **consistent with the resident rights set forth at §483.10(c)(2) and §483.10(c)(3),** that includes measurable objectives and time**frames** to meet a resident's medical, nursing, and mental and psychosocial needs that are identified in the comprehensive assessment. The comprehensive care plan must describe the following —

- (i) The services that are to be furnished to attain or maintain the resident's highest practicable physical, mental, and psychosocial well-being as required under **§483.24,** §483.25 **or §483.40;** and

- (ii) Any services that would otherwise be required under **§483.24,** §483.25 **or §483.40** but are not provided due to the resident's exercise of rights under §483.10, including the right to refuse treatment under §483.10**(c)(6).**

- *(iii) Any specialized services or specialized rehabilitative services the nursing facility will provide as a result of PASARR recommendations. If a facility disagrees with the findings of the PASARR, it must indicate its rationale in the resident's medical record.*
- *In consultation with the resident and the resident's representative(s)—*
  - *(A) The resident's goals for admission and desired outcomes.*
  - *(B) The resident's preference and potential for future discharge. Facilities must document whether the resident's desire to return to the community was assessed and any referrals to local contact agencies and/or other appropriate entities, for this purpose.*
  - *(C) Discharge plans in the comprehensive care plan, as appropriate, in accordance with the requirements set forth in paragraph (c) of this section.*

INTENT §483.21(b)

Each resident will have a person-centered comprehensive care plan developed and implemented to meet his other preferences and goals, and address the resident's medical, physical, mental and psychosocial needs.

DEFINITIONS §483.21(b)

"Resident's Goal":

The resident's desired outcomes and preferences for admission, which guide decision making during care planning.

"Interventions":

Actions, treatments, procedures, or activities designed to meet an objective.

"Measurable":

The ability to be evaluated or quantified.

"Objective":

A statement describing the results to be achieved to meet the resident's goals

"Person-centered care":

means to focus on the resident as the locus of control and support the resident in making their own choices and having control over their daily lives.

GUIDANCE: EXERPTS FROM THE SURVEYOR'S GUIDELINES

Through the care planning process, facility staff must work with the resident and his/her representative, if applicable, to understand and meet the resident's preferences, choices and goals during their stay at the facility. The facility must establish, document and implement the care and services to be provided to each resident to assist in attaining or maintaining his or her highest practicable quality of life. Care planning drives the type of care and services that a resident receives. If care planning is not complete, or is inadequate, the consequences may negatively impact the resident's quality of life, as well as the quality of care and services received.

Facilities are required to develop care plans that describe the resident's medical, nursing, physical, mental and psychosocial needs and preferences and how the facility will assist in meeting these needs and preferences. Care plans must include person-specific, measurable objectives and timeframes in order to evaluate the resident's progress toward his/her goal(s).

Care plans must be person-centered and reflect the resident's goals for admission and desired outcomes. Person-centered care means the facility focuses on the resident as the center of control, and supports each resident in making his or her own choices. Person-centered care includes making an effort to understand what each resident is communicating, verbally and nonverbally, identifying what is important to each resident with regard to daily routines and preferred activities, and having an understanding of the resident's life before coming to reside in the nursing home.

F657— Care Plan Timing and Revision

FOR VOICES FOR QUALITY CARE ADVOCATE

The regulations for this F-Tag are identical to those for F656. For further information see the Surveyor's Guidelines.

https://www.cms.gov/Medicare/Provider-Enrollment-and-Certification/GuidanceforLawsAndRegulations/Downloads/Advance-Appendix-PP-Including-Phase-2-.pdf

###

F658—Services Provided to Meet Professional Standards

FOR VOICES FOR QUALITY CARE ADVOCATE

For information on determining qualifications see the Surveyor's Guidelines under this F-Tag.

https://www.cms.gov/Medicare/Provider-Enrollment-and-Certification/GuidanceforLawsAndRegulations/Downloads/Advance-Appendix-PP-Including-Phase-2-.pdf

THE REGULATIONS

§483.21(b)(3) Comprehensive Care Plans

The services provided or arranged by the facility, *as outlined by the comprehensive care plan*, must—

- (i) Meet professional standards of quality.

###

F659—Qualified Persons

FOR VOICES FOR QUALITY CARE ADVOCATE

NOTE: the requirement that qualified persons must be culturally—competent and trauma—informed will not go into effect until 11/28/19!

THE REGULATIONS

§483.21(b)(3) Comprehensive Care Plans

The services provided or arranged by the facility, *as outlined by the comprehensive care plan*, must—

Be provided by qualified persons in accordance with each resident's written plan of care.

(iii) Be culturally-competent and trauma—informed.

[§483.21(b)(iii) will be implemented beginning November 28, 2019 (Phase 3)]

###

F660—Discharge Planning Process

FOR VOICES FOR QUALITY CARE ADVOCATE

Discharge Planning Conferences are extremely important for people moving to in-home care. See the Voices Handbook for a printable list of suggested items to consider. The continuation of pharmacy services is of particular importance.

THE REGULATIONS

§483.21(c)(1) Discharge Planning Process

The facility must develop and implement an effective discharge planning process that focuses on the resident's discharge goals, the preparation of residents to be active partners and effectively transition them to post-discharge care, and the reduction of factors leading to preventable readmissions. The facility's discharge planning process must be consistent with the discharge rights set forth at 483.15(b) as applicable and—

- *(i) Ensure that the discharge needs of each resident are identified and result in the development of a discharge plan for each resident.*
- *(ii) Include regular re-evaluation of residents to identify changes that require modification of the discharge plan. The discharge plan must be updated, as needed, to reflect these changes.*
- *(iii) Involve the interdisciplinary team, as defined by §483.21(b)(2)(ii), in the ongoing process of developing the discharge plan.*
- *(iv) Consider caregiver/support person availability and the resident's or caregiver's/support person(s) capacity and capability to perform required care, as part of the identification of discharge needs.*

- *(v) Involve the resident and resident representative in the development of the discharge plan and inform the resident and resident representative of the final plan.*
- *(vi) Address the resident's goals of care and treatment preferences.*
- *(vii) Document that a resident has been asked about their interest in receiving information regarding returning to the community.*
    - *(A) If the resident indicates an interest in returning to the community, the facility must document any referrals to local contact agencies or other appropriate entities made for this purpose.*
    - *(B) Facilities must update a resident's comprehensive care plan and discharge plan, as appropriate, in response to information received from referrals to local contact agencies or other appropriate entities.*
    - *(C) If discharge to the community is determined to not be feasible, the facility must document who made the determination and why.*

For residents who are transferred to another SNF or who are discharged to a HHA, IRF, or LTCH, assist residents and their resident representatives in selecting a post- acute care provider by using data that includes, but is not limited to SNF, HHA, IRF, or LTCH standardized patient assessment data, data on quality measures, and data on resource use to the extent the data is available. The facility must ensure that the post- acute care standardized patient assessment data, data on quality measures, and data on resource use is relevant and applicable to the resident's goals of care and treatment preferences.

- *(viii) Document, complete on a timely basis based on the resident's needs, and include in the clinical record, the evaluation of the resident's discharge needs and discharge plan. The results of the evaluation must be discussed with the resident or resident's representative. All relevant resident information must be incorporated.*

INTENT §483.21(c)(1)

This requirement intends to ensure that the facility has a discharge planning process in place which addresses each resident's discharge goals and needs, including caregiver support and referrals to local contact agencies, as appropriate, and involves the resident and if applicable, the resident representative and the interdisciplinary team in developing the discharge plan.

DEFINITIONS §483.21(c)(1)

"Discharge Planning":

A process that generally begins on admission and involves identifying each resident's discharge goals and needs, developing and implementing interventions to address them, and continuously evaluating them throughout the resident's stay to ensure a successful discharge.

"Home Health Agency (HHA)":

a public agency or private organization (or a subdivision of either) which is primarily engaged in providing skilled nursing services and other therapeutic services in the patient's home and meets the requirements of sections 1861(o) and 1891 of the Social Security Act.

"Inpatient Rehabilitation Facility (IRF)":

are freestanding rehabilitation hospitals or rehabilitation units in acute care hospitals that serve an inpatient population requiring intensive services for treatment.

"Local Contact Agency":

refers to each State's designated community contact agencies that can provide individuals with information about community living options and available supports and services. These local contact agencies may be a single entry point agency, such as an Aging and Disability Resource Center (ADRC), an Area Agency on Aging (AAA), a Center for Independent Living (CIL), or other state designated entities.

"Long Term Care Hospital (LTCH)":

are certified as acute-care hospitals, but focus on patients who, on average, stay more than 25 days. Many of the patients in LTCHs are transferred there from an intensive or critical care unit. LTCHs specialize in treating patients who may have more than one serious condition, but who may improve with time and care, and return home.

"Patient Assessment Data":

standardized, publicly available information derived from a post- acute care provider's patient/resident assessment instrument, e.g., Minimum Data Set (MDS), Outcome and Assessment Information Set (OASIS)

GUIDANCE: EXERPTS FROM THE SURVEYOR'S GUIDELINES §483.21(c)(1)

Discharge Planning

Discharge planning is the process of creating an individualized discharge care plan, which is part of the comprehensive care plan. It involves the interdisciplinary team (as defined in §483.21(b)(2)(ii) working with the resident and resident representative, if applicable, to develop interventions to meet the resident's discharge goals and needs to ensure a smooth and safe transition from the facility to the post-discharge setting. Discharge planning begins at admission and is based on the resident's assessment and *goals for care, desire to be discharged, and the resident's capacity for discharge. It also includes* identifying changes in the resident's condition, which may impact the discharge plan, warranting revisions to interventions. A well- executed discharge planning process, without avoidable complications, maximizes each resident's potential to improve, to the extent possible, based on his or her clinical condition. An inadequate discharge planning process may complicate the resident's recovery, lead to admission to a hospital, or even result in the resident's death.

The discharge care plan is part of the comprehensive care plan and must:

- *Be developed by the interdisciplinary team and involve direct communication with the resident and if applicable, the resident representative;*
- *Address the resident's goals for care and treatment preferences;*
- *Identify needs that must be addressed before the resident can be discharged, such as resident education, rehabilitation, and caregiver support and education;*
- *Be re-evaluated regularly and updated when the resident's needs or goals change;*
- *Document the resident's interest in, and any referrals made to the local contact agency;*
- *Identify post-discharge needs such as nursing and therapy services, medical equipment or modifications to the home, or ADL assistance.*

###

F661—Discharge Summary

THE REGULATIONS

§483.21(c)(2) Discharge Summary

When the facility anticipates discharge, a resident must have a discharge summary that includes, **but is not limited to, the following:**

- *(i)* A recapitulation of the resident's stay *that includes, but is not limited to, diagnoses, course of illness/treatment or therapy, and pertinent lab, radiology, and consultation results.*

- *(ii)* A final summary of the resident's status to include items in paragraph *(b)(1) of §483.20*, at the time of the discharge that is available for release to authorized persons and agencies, with the consent of the resident or resident's representative.

- (iii) *Reconciliation of all pre-discharge medications with the resident's post-discharge medications (both prescribed and over-the-counter).*

- (iv) A post-discharge plan of care that is developed with the participation of the resident and, *with the resident's consent, the resident representative(s)*, which will assist the resident to adjust to his or her new living environment. *The post-discharge plan of care must indicate where the individual plans to reside, any arrangements that have been made for the resident's follow up care and any post-discharge medical and non- medical services.*

INTENT of §483.21(c)(2)

To ensure the facility communicates necessary information to the resident, continuing care provider and other authorized persons at the time of an anticipated discharge.

DEFINITIONS §483.21(c)(2)

"Anticipated Discharge":

A discharge that is planned and not due to the resident's death or an emergency (e.g., hospitalization for an acute condition or emergency evacuation).

"Continuing Care Provider":

The entity or person who will assume responsibility for the resident's care after discharge. This includes licensed facilities, agencies, physicians, practitioners, and/or other licensed caregivers.

"Recapitulation of Stay":

A concise summary of the resident's stay and course of treatment in the facility.

"Reconciliation of Medications":

A process of comparing pre-discharge medications to post- discharge medications by creating an accurate list of both prescription and over the counter medications that includes the drug name, dosage, frequency, route, and indication for use for the purpose of preventing unintended changes or omissions at transition points in care.

#

483.24 Quality of Life

F675—Quality of Life

THE REGULATIONS

§ 483.24 Quality of life

Quality of life is a fundamental principle that applies to all care and services provided to facility residents. Each resident must receive and the facility must provide the necessary care and services to attain or maintain the highest practicable physical, mental, and psychosocial well-being, *consistent with the resident's* comprehensive assessment and plan of care.

DEFINITIONS

"Person Centered Care" –

For the purposes of this subpart, person-centered care means to focus on the resident as the locus of control and support the resident in making their own choices and having control over their daily lives. (Definitions - §483.5)

"Pervasive"

For the purposes of this guidance, pervasive means spread through or embedded within every part of something.

"Quality of Life" An individual's "

sense of well-being, level of satisfaction with life and feeling of self-worth and self-esteem. For nursing home residents, this includes a basic sense of satisfaction with oneself, the environment, the care received, the accomplishments of desired goals, and control over one's life."

INTENT

The intent of this requirement is to specify the facility's responsibility to create and sustain an environment that humanizes and individualizes each resident's quality of life by:

- *Ensuring all staff, across all shifts and departments, understand the principles of quality of life, and honor and support these principles for each resident; and Ensuring that the care and services provided are person-centered, and honor and support each resident's preferences, choices, values and beliefs.*

-

GUIDANCE: EXERPTS FROM THE SURVEYOR'S GUIDELINES

According to the 1986 Institute of Medicine (IOM) published report "Improving the Quality of Care in Nursing Homes," principles of Quality of Life included:

- *A sense of well-being, satisfaction with life, and feeling of self-worth and self-esteem; and*
- *A sense of satisfaction with oneself, the environment, the care received, the accomplishments of desired goals, and control over one's life.*

.....for determining whether a resident's quality of life is being supported and or enhanced. Refer to this link for the entire IOM report: https://www.ncbi.nlm.nih.gov/books/NBK217548/#ddd0003 7

###

F676—Activities of Daily Living (ADL'S)/ Maintain Abilities

THE REGULATIONS

§483.24(a) *Based on the comprehensive assessment of a resident and consistent with the resident's needs and choices, the facility must provide the necessary care and services to ensure that a* resident's abilities in activities of daily living do not diminish unless circumstances of the individual's clinical condition demonstrate that such diminution was unavoidable. This includes *the facility ensuring that:*

§483.24(a)(1) A resident is given the appropriate treatment and services to maintain or improve his or her *ability to carry out the activities of daily living, including those specified in paragraph (b) of this section ...*

§483.24(b) Activities of daily living. The facility must provide care and services in accordance with paragraph (a) for the following activities of daily living:

§483.24(b)(1) *Hygiene* –bathing, dressing, grooming, *and oral care,*

§483.24(b)(2) *Mobility*—transfer and ambulation, *including walking,*

§483.24(b)(3) *Elimination*-toileting,

§483.24(b)(4) *Dining*-eating, including meals and snacks,

§483.24(b)(5) *Communication, including*

- (i) Speech,
- (ii) Language,
- (iii) Other functional communication systems.

###

F677—ADL Care Provided for Dependent Residents

FOR VOICES FOR QUALITY CARE ADVOCATES

The Advocate should be particularly attentive to situations in which needed care loses out to convenience for staff.

THE REGULATIONS

§483.24(a)(2) A resident who is unable to carry out activities of daily living receives the necessary services to maintain good nutrition, grooming, and personal and oral hygiene; and

DEFINITIONS

"Oral care"

> refers to the maintenance of a healthy mouth, which includes not only teeth, but the lips, gums, and supporting tissues. This involves not only activities such as brushing of teeth or oral appliances, but also maintenance of oral mucosa.

"Speech, language or other functional communication systems"

> refers to the resident's ability to effectively communicate requests, needs, opinions, and urgent problems; to express emotion, to listen to others and to participate in social conversation whether in speech, writing, gesture, behavior, or a combination of these (e.g., a communication board or electronic augmentative communication device).

"Assistance with the bathroom"

refers to the resident's ability to use the toilet room (or commode, bedpan, urinal); transfer on/off the toilet, clean themselves, change absorbent pads or briefs, manage ostomy or catheter, and adjust clothes.

"Transfer"

refers to resident's ability to move between surfaces - to/from: bed, chair, wheelchair, and standing positions. (Excludes to/from bath/toilet.)

GUIDANCE: EXERPTS FROM THE SURVEYOR'S GUIDELINES

The ***existence*** of a clinical diagnosis shall not justify a decline in a resident's ability to perform ADLs unless the resident's clinical picture reflects the normal progression of the disease/ condition has resulted in an unavoidable decline in the resident's ability to perform ADLs. Conditions which may demonstrate an unavoidable decline in the resident's ability to perform ADLs include but are not limited to the following:

- The natural progression of ***a debilitating*** disease ***with known funtional decline;***
- The onset of ***an acute episode causing*** physical or mental disability while the ***resident is*** receiving care to restore or maintain functional abilities; and
- The resident's or his/her representative's decision to refuse care and treatment to restore or maintain functional abilities after efforts by the facility to ***inform and educate about the benefits/risks of the proposed care and treatment;*** counsel and/or offer alternatives to the resident or representative. ***The decision to***

185

refuse care and treatment must be documented in the clinical record. *Documentation must include* interventions identified on the care plan and *in place to* minimize or decrease functional loss that were refused by the *resident or resident's representative* and any interventions that were substituted *with consent of the resident and/or representative* to minimize further decline. *NOTE: In some cases, residents with dementia may resist the manner in which care is being provided, or attempted, which can be misinterpreted as declination of care. In some cases the resident with dementia does not understand what is happening, or may be fearful of unfamiliar staff, or may be anxious or frustrated due to inability to communicate. Facility staff are responsible to attempt to identify the underlying cause of the "refusal/declination" of care.*

F678—Cardio-Pulmonary Resuscitation (CPR)

THE REGULATIONS

§483.24(a)(3) Personnel provide basic life support, including CPR, to a resident requiring such emergency care prior to the arrival of emergency medical personnel and subject to related physician orders and the resident's advance directives.

DEFINITIONS

"Advance directive"

is defined as a written instruction, such as a living will or durable power of attorney for health care, recognized under State law (whether statutory or as recognized by the courts of the State), relating to the provision of health care when the individual is incapacitated. 42 C.F.R. §489.100. Some States also recognize a documented oral instruction.

"Basic life support"

is a level of medical care which is used for victims of life-threatening illnesses or injuries until they can be given full medical care at a hospital, and may include recognition of sudden cardiac arrest, activiation of the emergency response system, early cardiopulmonary resuscitation, and rapid defibrillation with an automatied external defibrillator, if available.

"Cardiopulmonary resuscitation (CPR)"

refers to any medical intervention used to restore circulatory and/or respiratory function that has ceased.

"Code Status"

refers to the level of medical interventions a person wishes to have started if their heart or breathing stops.

"Do Not Resuscitate(DNR) Order"

refers to a medical order issued by a physician or other authorized non-physician practitioner that directs healthcare providers not to administer CPR in the event of cardiac or respiratory arrest. Existence of an advance directive does not imply that a resident has a DNR order. The medical record should show evidence of documented discussions leading to a DNR order.

INTENT

To ensure that each facility is able to and does provide emergency basic life support immediately when needed, including cardiopulmonary resuscitation (CPR), to any resident requiring such care prior to the arrival of emergency medical personnel in accordance with related physicians orders, such as DNRs, and the resident's advance directives.

GUIDANCE: EXERPTS FROM THE SURVEYOR'S GUIDELINES

See the Surveyor's Guidelines for additional information.

https://www.cms.gov/Medicare/Provider-Enrollment-and-Certification/GuidanceforLawsAndRegulations/Downloads/Advance-Appendix-PP-Including-Phase-2-.pdf

#

F679—Activities Meet Interest/Needs of Each Resident

FOR VOICES FOR QUALITY CARE ADVOCATES

Activities is an essential part of life in a nursing home. One of the main issues in nursing home life is the oppressive boredom. CMS still has not defined this section as clearly and expansively as we'd like.

THE REGULATIONS

§483.24(c) Activities.

§483.24(c)(1) The facility must provide, **based on the comprehensive assessment and care plan and the preferences of each resident**, an ongoing **program to support residents in their choice** of activities, **both facility-sponsored group and individual activities** and independent activities, designed to meet the interests **of** and **support** the physical, mental, and psychosocial well-being of each resident, **encouraging both independence and interaction in the community.**

DEFINITIONS

"Activities"

refer to any endeavor, other than routine ADLs, in which a resident participates that is intended to enhance her/his sense of well-being and to promote or enhance physical, cognitive, and emotional health. These include, but are not limited to, activities that promote self-esteem, pleasure, comfort, education, creativity, success, and independence.

NOTE: ADL-related activities, such as manicures/pedicures, hair styling, and makeovers, may be considered part of the activities program.

GUIDANCE: EXERPTS FROM THE SURVEYOR'S GUIDELINES

Research findings and the observations of positive resident outcomes confirm that activities are an integral component of residents' lives. Residents have indicated that daily life and involvement should be meaningful. Activities are meaningful when they reflect a person's interests and lifestyle, are enjoyable to the person, help the person to feel useful, and provide a sense of belonging. *Maintaining contact and interaction with the community is an important aspect of a person's well-being and facilitates feelings of connectedness and self- esteem. Involvement in community includes interactions such as assisting the resident to maintain his/her ability to independently shop, attend the community theater, local concerts, library, and participate in community groups.*

###

F680—Qualifications of Activity Professional

THE REGULATIONS

§483.24(c)(2) The activities program must be directed by a qualified professional who is a qualified therapeutic recreation specialist or an activities professional who—

- (i) Is licensed or registered, if applicable, by the State in which practicing; and
- (ii) Is:
  - o *(A)* Eligible for certification as a therapeutic recreation specialist or as an activities professional by a recognized accrediting body on or after October 1, 1990; or
  - o *(B)* Has 2 years of experience in a social or recreational program within the last 5 years, one of which was full-time in a therapeutic activities program; or
  - o *(C)* Is a qualified occupational therapist or occupational therapy assistant; or
  - o *(D)* Has completed a training course approved by the State.

DEFINITIONS

"Recognized accrediting body"

refers to those organizations that certify, register, or license therapeutic recreation specialists, activity professionals, or occupational therapists.

###

483.25 Quality of Care

F684—Quality of Care

THE REGULATIONS

Quality of care is a fundamental principle that applies to all treatment and care provided to facility residents. Based on the comprehensive assessment *of a resident, the facility must ensure that* residents receive *treatment and* care *in accordance with professional standards of practice, the comprehensive person-centered care plan, and the residents' choices, including but not limited to the following:*

###

F685—Treatment/Devices to Maintain Hearing/Vision

FOR VOICES FOR QUALITY CARE ADVOCATES

This is a continual issue for many advocates but it is one that is very often overlooked. Diminished vision and hearing can have profound impacts upon quality of life and various personality factors. A hearing loss is a socially isolating condition that promotes paranoia and confusion in addition to eliminating many of life's recreational and other pleasures. It can also interfere with care factors and health diagnoses if the individual is unable to clearly hear questions from providers and others.

Unfortunately, at this time, there are few good solutions for people who enter a nursing home without hearing aids unless they have family members who can pay for them. It is possible, with considerable advocacy, to persuade Medicaid to actually pay for both glasses and hearing aids but it often takes strong and consistent advocacy from everyone involved.

Check the internet also. There are often organizations or hearing aid manufacturers who will provide assistance but these tend to alter from time to time. Glasses are somewhat easier to obtain since they carry a much lower price tag.

THE REGULATIONS

§483.25*(a)* Vision and hearing

To ensure that residents receive proper treatment and assistive devices to maintain vision and hearing abilities, the facility must, if necessary, assist the resident—

§483.25*(a)(1)* In making appointments, and

§483.25*(a)(2)* By arranging for transportation to and from the office of a practitioner specializing in the treatment of vision or hearing impairment or the office of a professional specializing in the provision of vision or hearing assistive devices.

DEFINITIONS

Assistive devices to maintain vision include, **but are not limited to,** glasses, contact lenses, magnifying **lens or other devices that are used by the resident.**

Assistive devices to maintain hearing include, **but are not limited to**, hearing aids, **and amplifiers**.

GUIDANCE: EXERPTS FROM THE SURVEYOR'S GUIDELINES

This requirement does not mean that the facility must provide refraction, glasses, contact lenses **or other assistive devices**, conduct comprehensive audiological evaluations (**other than the screening that is** a part of the required assessment in §483.20(b)) or provide hearing aids **or other devices.**

The facility's responsibility is to assist residents and their **representatives** in locating and utilizing any available resources (e.g., Medicare or Medicaid program payment, local health organizations offering items and services which are available free to the community) for the provision of the services the resident needs. This includes making appointments and arranging transportation to obtain needed services.

In situations where the resident has lost their device, facilities must assist residents and their representative in locating resources, as well as in making appointments, and arranging for transportation to replace the lost devices.

###

194

F686—Treatment/Services to Prevent/Heal Pressure Ulcers

FOR VOICES FOR QUALITY CARE ADVOCATES

Pressure Ulcers are a vast and complicated issue. An advocate will need to look beyond the material we are including here. Consult the Surveyor's Guidelines where there is a considerable amount of additional information. Also, an internet search for recent postings will provide the latest medical interventions.

There are many other remedies available these days including maggot therapy. It does sound disgusting but in many cases it is extremely effective in avoiding surgery. One caution, however, is that with proper treatment, pressure ulcers should never occur at any time other than a short time before death when all bodily systems start to break down. Other than that, there is no excuse for pressure ulcers and they are regarded by CMS as "never events".

THE REGULATIONS

§483.25(b) *Skin Integrity*

§483.25(b)(1) Pressure *ulcers.*

Based on the comprehensive assessment of a resident, the facility must ensure that—

- (i) *A resident receives care, consistent with professional standards of practice, to prevent pressure ulcers and* does not develop pressure ulcers unless the individual's clinical condition demonstrates that they were unavoidable; and

- (ii) A resident *with* pressure *ulcers* receives necessary treatment and services, *consistent with professional standards of practice*, to promote healing, prevent infection and prevent new ulcers from developing.

DEFINITIONS

"Pressure Ulcer/Injury (PU/PI)"

refers to localized damage to the skin and/or underlying soft tissue usually over a bony prominence or related to a medical or other device. A pressure injury will present as intact skin and may be painful. A pressure ulcer will present as an open ulcer, the appearance of which will vary depending on the stage and may be painful. The injury occurs as a result of intense and/or prolonged pressure or pressure in combination with shear. The tolerance of soft tissue for pressure and shear may also be affected by skin temperature and moisture, nutrition, perfusion, co-morbidities and condition of the soft tissue.

Avoidable/Unavoidable

- "**Avoidable**" means that the resident developed a *pressure ulcer/injury* and that the facility did not do one or more of the following: evaluate the resident's clinical condition and risk factors; define and implement interventions that are consistent with resident needs, resident goals, and *professional* standards of practice; monitor and evaluate the impact of the interventions; or revise the interventions as appropriate.

- "**Unavoidable**" means that the resident developed a *pressure ulcer/injury* even though the facility had evaluated the resident's clinical condition and risk factors; defined and implemented interventions that are consistent with resident needs, goals, and *professional* standards of practice; monitored and evaluated the impact of the interventions; and revised the approaches as appropriate.

Colonized/Infected

- "**Colonized**" refers to the presence of micro-organisms on the surface or in the tissue of a wound without the signs and symptoms of an infection.

196

- **"Infected"** refers to the presence of micro-organisms in sufficient quantity to overwhelm the defenses of viable tissues and produce the signs and symptoms of infection.

Debridement-

Debridement is the removal of devitalized/necrotic tissue and foreign matter from a wound to improve or facilitate the healing process. Debridement methods may include a range of treatments such as the use of enzymatic dressings to surgical debridement in order to remove tissue or matter from a wound to promote healing.

Eschar/Slough

- *"Eschar" is dead or devitalized tissue that is hard or soft in texture; usually black, brown, or tan in color, and may appear scab-like. Necrotic tissue and eschar are usually firmly adherent to the base of the wound and often the sides/ edges of the wound.*
- *"Slough" is non-viable yellow, tan, gray, green or brown tissue; usually moist, can be soft, stringy and mucinous in texture. Slough may be adherent to the base of the wound or present in clumps throughout the wound bed*

Exudate

- **"Exudate"** is any fluid that has been forced out of the tissues or its capillaries because of inflammation or injury. It may contain serum, cellular debris, bacteria and leukocytes.
- **"Purulent exudate/drainage/discharge"** is any product of inflammation that contains pus (e.g., leukocytes, bacteria, and liquefied necrotic debris).
- **"Serous drainage or exudate"** is watery, clear, or slightly yellow/tan/pink fluid that has separated from the blood and presents as drainage.

Friction/Shearing

- **"Friction"** is the mechanical force exerted on skin that is dragged across any surface.

- **"Shearing"** occurs when layers of skin rub against each other or when the skin remains stationary and the underlying tissue moves and stretches and angulates or tears the underlying capillaries and blood vessels causing tissue damage.

Granulation Tissue - "Granulation tissue" is the pink-red moist tissue that fills an open wound, when it starts to heal. It contains new blood vessels, collagen, fibroblasts, and inflammatory cells.

Tissue tolerance

is the ability of the skin and its supporting structures to endure the effects of pressure, without adverse effects. Tissue tolerance affects the length of time a resident can maintain a position without suffering a pressure ulcer/injury.

Tunnel/Sinus Tract/Undermining - The terms tunnel and sinus tract are often used interchangeably.

- A **"tunnel"** is a passageway of tissue destruction under the skin surface that has an opening at the skin level from the edge of the wound.
- A **"sinus tract"** is a cavity or channel underlying a wound that involves an area larger than the visible surface of the wound.
- **"Undermining"** is the destruction of tissue or ulceration extending under the skin edges (margins) so that the pressure ulcer is larger at its base than at the skin surface. Undermining often develops from shearing forces and is differentiated from tunneling by the larger extent of the wound edge involved and the absence of a channel or tract extending from the pressure ulcer under the adjacent intact skin.

INTENT

The intent of this requirement is that the resident does not develop pressure **ulcers/injuries (PU/PIs)** unless clinically unavoidable and that the facility provides care and services consistent with professional standards of practice to:

- Promote the prevention of pressure **ulcer/injury** development;
- Promote the healing of existing pressure **ulcers/injuries** (including prevention of infection to the extent possible); and
- Prevent development of additional pressure **ulcer/injury**.

GUIDANCE: EXERPTS FROM THE SURVEYOR'S

NOTE: Blanchable refers to a red area that loses its reddness when pressed. A non-blanchable red area would remain red when pressed.

Stage 1 Pressure Injury: Non-blanchable erythema of intact skin

Intact skin with a localized area of non-blanchable erythema (redness). In darker skin tones, the PI may appear with persistent red, blue, or purple hues. The presence of blanchable erythema or changes in sensation, temperature, or firmness may precede visual changes. Color changes of intact skin may also indicate a deep tissue PI (see below).

Stage 2 Pressure Ulcer: Partial-thickness skin loss with exposed dermis

Partial-thickness loss of skin with exposed dermis, presenting as a shallow open ulcer. The wound bed is viable, pink or red, moist, and may also present as an intact or open/ruptured blister. Adipose (fat) is not visible and deeper tissues are not visible. Granulation tissue, slough and eschar are not present. This stage should not be used to describe moisture associated skin damage including incontinence associated dermatitis, intertriginous dermatitis (inflammation of skin folds), medical adhesive related skin injury, or traumatic wounds (skin tears, burns, abrasions).

Stage 3 Pressure Ulcer: Full-thickness skin loss

Full-thickness loss of skin, in which subcutaneous fat may be visible in the ulcer and granulation tissue and epibole (rolled wound edges) are often present. Slough and/or eschar may be visible but does not obscure the depth of tissue loss. The depth of tissue damage varies by anatomical location; areas of significant adiposity can develop deep wounds. Undermining and tunneling may occur. Fascia, muscle, tendon, ligament, cartilage and/or bone are not exposed. If slough or eschar obscures the wound bed, it is an Unstageable PU/PI.

Stage 4 Pressure Ulcer: Full-thickness skin and tissue loss

Full-thickness skin and tissue loss with exposed or directly palpable fascia, muscle, tendon, ligament, cartilage or bone in the ulcer. Slough and/or eschar may be visible on some parts of the wound bed. Epibole (rolled edges), undermining and/or tunneling often occur. Depth varies by anatomical location. If slough or eschar obscures the wound bed, it is an unstageable PU/PI.

Unstageable Pressure Ulcer: Obscured full-thickness skin and tissue loss

Full-thickness skin and tissue loss in which the extent of tissue damage within the ulcer cannot be confirmed because the wound bed is obscured by slough or eschar. Stable eschar (i.e. dry, adherent, intact without erythema or fluctuance) should only be removed after careful clinical consideration and consultation with the resident's physician, or nurse practitioner, physician assistant, or clinical nurse specialist if allowable under state licensure laws. If the slough or eschar is removed, a Stage 3 or Stage 4 pressure ulcer will be revealed. If the anatomical depth of the tissue damage involved can be determined, then the reclassified stage should be assigned. The pressure ulcer does not have to be completely debrided or free of all slough or eschar for reclassification of stage to occur.

Other staging considerations include:

Deep Tissue Pressure Injury (DTPI): Persistent non-blanchable deep red, maroon or purple discoloration

Intact skin with localized area of persistent non-blanchable deep red, maroon, purple discoloration due to damage of underlying soft tissue.. This area may be preceded by tissue that is painful, firm, mushy, boggy, warmer or cooler as compared to adjacent tissue. These changes often precede skin color changes and discoloration may appear differently in darkly pigmented skin. This injury results from intense and/or prolonged pressure and shear forces at the bone-muscle interface. The wound may evolve rapidly

F687—Foot Care

THE REGULATIONS

§483.25(b)(2) Foot care.

To ensure that residents receive proper treatment and care to maintain mobility and good foot health, the facility must:

Provide foot care and treatment, in accordance with professional standards of practice, including to prevent complications from the resident's medical condition(s) and

- *If necessary, assist the resident in making appointments with a qualified person, and arranging for transportation to and from such appointments.*

GUIDANCE: EXERPTS FROM THE SURVEYOR'S GUIDELINES

Facilities are responsible for providing the necessary treatment and foot care to residents. Treatment also includes preventive care to avoid podiatric complications in residents with diabetes and circulatory disorders who are prone to developing foot problems. Foot care that is provided in the facility, such as toe nail clipping for residents without complicating disease processes, must be provided by staff who have received education and training to provide this service within professional standards of practice. Residents requiring foot care who have complicating disease processes must be referred to qualified professionals as listed below.

Facilities are also responsible for providing residents access to qualified professionals who can treat foot disorders, by making necessary appointments and arranging transportation. Examples include podiatrist, Doctor of Medicine, and Doctor of Osteopathy. ***Foot disorders which may require treatment include***, but are not limited to: corns, neuromas, calluses, ***hallux valgus*** (bunions), ***digiti flexus (hammertoe),*** heel spurs, and nail disorders. ***The facility is also responsible for assisting residents in making appointments and arranging transportation to obtain needed services.***

###

F688—Increase/Prevent Decrease in Range of Motion/Mobility

FOR VOICES FOR QUALITY CARE ADVOCATES

Advocates should watch for non-compliances here. We often encounter limited or a total lack of range of motion exercises. This can lead to permanent incapacities including "frozen" muscles in hands.

THE REGULATIONS

§483.25*(c) Mobility.*

§483.25*(c)*(1) The facility must ensure that a resident who enters the facility without limited range of motion does not experience reduction in range of motion unless the resident's clinical condition demonstrates that a reduction in range of motion is unavoidable; and

§483.25*(c)*(2) A resident with limited range of motion receives appropriate treatment and services to increase range of motion and/or to prevent further decrease in range of motion.

§483.25(c)(3) A resident with limited mobility receives appropriate services, equipment, and assistance to maintain or improve mobility with the maximum practicable independence unless a reduction in mobility is demonstrably unavoidable.

DEFINITIONS

"Active ROM"

means the performance of an exercise to move a joint without any assistance or effort of another person to the muscles surrounding the joint.

"Active Assisted ROM"

means the use of the muscles surrounding the joint to perform the exercise but requires some help from the therapist or equipment (such as a strap).

Mobility refers to all types of movement, including walking, movement in a bed, transferring from a bed to a chair, all with or without assistance or moving about an area either with or without an appliance (chair, walker, cane, crutches, etc.).

"Muscle atrophy"

means the wasting or loss of muscle tissue.

"Passive ROM"

means the movement of a joint through the range of motion with no effort from the patient.

"Range of motion (ROM)"

means the full movement potential of a joint.

INTENT

The intent of this regulation *(F688)* is to ensure that *the facility provides the services, care and equipment to assure that:*

- *A resident maintains, and/or improves to his/her highest level of range of motion (ROM) and mobility, unless a reduction is clinically unavoidable; and*
- *A resident with limited range of motion and mobility maintains or improves function unless reduced Range of Motion (ROM)/mobility is unavoidable based on the resident's clinical condition.*

GUIDANCE: EXERPTS FROM THE SURVEYOR'S GUIDELINES

The resident's comprehensive assessment should include and measure, as appropriate, a resident's current extent of movement of his/her joints and the identification of limitations, if any and opportunities for improvement. The assessment should address whether the resident had previously received treatment and services for ROM and whether he/she maintained his/her ROM, whether the ROM declined, and why the treatment/services were stopped. In addition, the assessment should address, for a resident with limited ROM, if he/she is not receiving services, the reason for the services to not be provided..

The resident-specific, comprehensive assessment should identify individual risks which could impact the resident's range of motion including, but not limited to:

- *Immobilization (e.g., bedfast, reclining in a chair or remaining seated in a chair/wheelchair);*
- *Neurological conditions causing functional limitations such as cerebral vascular accidents, multiple sclerosis, Amyotrophic Lateral Sclerosis (ALS) or Lou Gehrig's disease, Guillain-Barre syndrome, Muscular Dystrophy, or cerebral palsy, etc.;*
- *Any condition where movement may result in pain, spasms or loss of movement such as cancer, presence of pressure ulcers, arthritis, gout, late stages of Alzheimer's, contractures, dependence on mechanical ventilation, etc.; or*
- *Clinical conditions such as immobilized limbs or digits because of injury, fractures, or surgical procedures including amputations.*

###

F689—Free of Accident Hazards/Supervision/Devices

THE REGULATIONS

§483.25(d) Accidents.

The facility must ensure that –

§483.25(d)(1) The resident environment remains as free of accident hazards as is possible; and

§483.25(d)(2)Each resident receives adequate supervision and assistance devices to prevent accidents.

DEFINITIONS

"Accident"

*refers to any unexpected or unintentional incident, which results or may result in injury or illness to a resident. This does not include **other types of harm, such as** adverse outcomes that are a direct consequence of treatment or care that is provided in accordance with current professional standards of practice (e.g., drug side effects or reaction).*

"Avoidable Accident"

means that an accident occurred because the facility failed to:

- Identify environmental hazards and/or *assess* individual resident risk of an accident, including the need for supervision *and/or assistive devices;* and/or

- Evaluate/analyze the hazards and risks *and eliminate them, if possible, or, if not possible, identify and implement measures to reduce the hazards/risks as much as possible*; and/or

- Implement interventions, including adequate supervision *and assistive devices,* consistent with a resident's needs, goals, *care plan* and current professional standards of practice in order to eliminate the risk, if possible, and, if not, reduce the risk of an accident; and/or

- Monitor the effectiveness of the interventions and modify the care plan as necessary, in accordance with current professional standards of practice.

"Unavoidable Accident"

means that an accident occurred despite **sufficient and comprehensive** facility systems **designed and implemented to:**

- Identify environmental hazards and individual resident risk of an accident, including the need for supervision; and

- Evaluate/analyze the hazards and risks **and eliminate them, if possible and, if not possible, reduce them as much as possible**;

- Implement interventions, including adequate supervision, consistent with the resident's needs, goals, care **plan**, and current professional standards of practice in order to **eliminate or** reduce the risk of an accident; and

- Monitor the effectiveness of the interventions and modify the interventions as necessary, in accordance with current professional standards of practice.

"Assistance Device or Assistive Device"

refers to any item (e.g., fixtures such as handrails, grab bars, and **mechanical** devices/equipment such as **stand- alone or overhead** transfer lifts, canes, wheelchairs, **and walkers**, etc.) that is used by, or in the care of a resident to promote, supplement, or enhance the resident's function and/or safety.

NOTE: The currently accepted nomenclature refers to "assistive devices." Although the term "assistance devices" is used in the regulation, the Guidance provided in this document will refer to "assistive devices."

"Environment"

refers to any environment or area in the facility that is frequented by or accessible to residents, including (but not limited to) the residents' rooms, bathrooms, hallways, dining areas, lobby, outdoor patios, therapy areas and activity areas.

"Fall"

refers to unintentionally coming to rest on the ground, floor, or other lower level, but not as a result of an overwhelming external force (e.g., resident pushes another resident). An episode where a resident lost his/her balance and would have fallen, *if not for another person or if he or she had not caught him/herself,* is considered a fall. A fall without injury is still a fall. Unless there is evidence suggesting otherwise, when a resident is found on the floor, a fall is considered to have occurred *(refer to Resident Assessment Instrument User's Manual. Version 3.0, Chapter 3, page J-27).*

"Hazards"

refer to elements of the resident environment that have the potential to cause injury or illness.

- "Hazards over which the facility has control" are those hazards in the resident environment where reasonable efforts by the facility could influence the risk for resulting injury or illness.

- "Free of accident hazards as is possible" refers to being free of accident hazards over which the facility has control.

"Position change alarms"

are alerting devices intended to monitor a resident's movement. The devices emit an audible signal when the resident moves in a certain way. Types of position change alarms include chair and bed sensor pads, bedside alarmed mats, alarms clipped to a resident's clothing, seatbelt alarms, and infrared beam motion detectors. 7 Position change alarms do not include alarms intended to monitor for unsafe wandering such as door or elevator alarms.

"Risk"

refers to any external factor, *facility characteristic (e.g., staffing or physical environment)* or characteristic of an individual resident that influences the likelihood of an accident.

"Supervision/Adequate Supervision"

refers to an intervention and means of mitigating the risk of an accident. Facilities are obligated to provide adequate supervision to prevent accidents. Adequate supervision is *determined by assessing the appropriate level and number of staff required, the competency and training of the staff, and the frequency of supervision needed. This determination is based on the* individual resident's assessed needs and identified hazards in the resident environment. Adequate supervision may vary from resident to resident and from time to time for the same resident.

INTENT

The intent of this requirement is to ensure the facility provides an environment that is free from accident hazards over which the facility has control and provides supervision and assistive devices to each resident to prevent avoidable accidents. This includes:

- Identifying hazard(s) and risk(s);
- Evaluating and analyzing hazard(s) and risk(s);
- Implementing interventions to reduce hazard(s) and risk(s); and
- Monitoring for effectiveness and modifying interventions when necessary.

GUIDANCE: EXERPTS FROM THE SURVEYOR'S GUIDELINES

See the Surveyor's Guidelines for more information. This is a small excerpt.

RISKS AND ENVIRONMENTAL HAZARDS

The physical plant, devices, and equipment described in this section may not be hazards by themselves but can become hazardous when a vulnerable resident interacts with them. Some temporary hazards in the resident environment can affect most residents who have access to them (e.g., construction, painting, and housekeeping activities). Other situations may be hazardous only for certain individuals (e.g., accessible smoking materials).

In order to be considered hazardous, an element of the resident environment must be accessible to a vulnerable resident. Resident vulnerability is based on risk factors including the individual resident's functional status, medical condition, cognitive abilities, mood, and health treatments (e.g., medications). Resident vulnerability to hazards may change over time. Ongoing assessment helps identify when elements in the environment pose hazards to a particular resident.

Certain sharp items, such as scissors, kitchen utensils, knitting needles, or other items, may be appropriate for many residents but hazardous for others with cognitive impairments. Handrails, assistive devices, and any surface that a resident may come in contact with may cause injury, if the surface is not in good condition, free from sharp edges or other hazards *or not installed properly.*

Improper actions or omissions by staff can create hazards in the physical plant (e.g., building and grounds), environment, and/or with devices and equipment. Examples of such hazards might include fire doors that have been propped open, disabled locks or latches, nonfunctioning alarms, buckled or badly torn carpets, cords on floors, irregular walking surfaces, improper storage and access to toxic chemicals, exposure to unsafe heating unit surfaces, and unsafe water temperatures. Other potential hazards may include furniture that is not appropriate for a resident (e.g., chairs or beds that are *not the proper height or width for the resident to transfer to and from safely* or unstable as to present a fall hazard) and lighting that is either inadequate or so intense as to create glare. Devices for resident care, such as pumps, ventilators, and assistive devices, may be hazardous when they are defective, disabled, or improperly used (i.e., used in a manner that is not per manufacturer's recommendations or current professional standards of practice).

###

F690—Bowel/Bladder Incontinence, Catheter, Urinary Tract Infections

THE REGULATIONS

§483.25*(e)* Incontinence.

§483.25*(e)*(1) **The facility must ensure that a resident who *is continent of bladder and bowel on admission receives services and assistance to maintain continence unless his or her clinical condition is or becomes such that continence is not possible to maintain.***

§483.25*(e)(2)For a resident with urinary incontinence, based on the resident's comprehensive assessment, the facility must ensure that—*

- (i) A resident who enters the facility without an indwelling catheter is not catheterized unless the resident's clinical condition demonstrates that catheterization was necessary;

- *(ii) A resident who enters the facility with an indwelling catheter or subsequently receives one is assessed for removal of the catheter as soon as possible unless the resident's clinical condition demonstrates that catheterization is necessary and*

- (iii) A resident who is incontinent of bladder receives appropriate treatment and services to prevent urinary tract infections and to restore *continence to the extent possible.*

§483.25*(e)(3) For a resident with fecal incontinence, based on the resident's comprehensive assessment, the facility must ensure that a resident who is incontinent of bowel receives appropriate treatment and services to restore as much normal bowel function as possible.*

DEFINITIONS

"Bacteremia"

is the presence of bacteria in the bloodstream.

"Bacteriuria"

is defined as the presence of bacteria in the urine.

"Continence"

refers to any void that occurs voluntarily, or as the result of prompted, assisted, or scheduled use of the bathroom.

"Sepsis"

is the body's overwhelming and life-threatening response to an infection which can lead to tissue damage, organ failure, and death.

"Urinary Incontinence"

is the involuntary loss or leakage of urine.

"Urinary Retention"

is the inability to completely empty the urinary bladder by micturition.

"Urinary Tract Infection (UTI)"

is a clinically detectable condition associated with invasion by disease causing microorganisms of some part of the urinary tract, including the urethra (urethritis), bladder (cystitis), ureters (ureteritis), and/or kidney (pyelonephritis). An infection of the urethra or bladder is classified as a lower tract UTI and infection involving the ureter or kidney is classified as an upper tract UTI.

INTENT

The intent of this requirement is to ensure that:

- *Each resident who is continent of bladder and bowel receives the necessary services and assistance to maintain continence, unless it is clinically not possible.*
- Each resident who is incontinent of urine is identified, assessed and provided appropriate treatment and services to achieve or maintain as much normal bladder function as possible;
- *A resident who is incontinent of bowel is identified, assessed and provided appropriate treatment and services to restore as much normal bowel function as possible;*
- An indwelling catheter is not used unless there is valid medical justification *for catheterization* and *the catheter* is discontinued as soon as clinically warranted;
- Services are provided to restore or improve normal bladder function to the extent possible, after the removal of the *indwelling* catheter; and
- A resident, with or without *an indwelling* catheter, receives the appropriate care and services to prevent *urinary tract* infections to the extent possible.

GUIDANCE: EXERPTS FROM THE SURVEYOR'S

Note: pages of information in the Surveyor's Guidelines.

A resident who is continent of bladder *on admission must receive care, including assistance, and services to maintain continence unless his/her clinical condition is or becomes such that continence is not possible to maintain. If a resident is admitted with incontinence of bladder, he/she* receives appropriate treatment and services to prevent urinary tract infections and to restore as much normal bladder function as possible.

#

F691—Colostomy, Urostomy, or Ileostomy Care

See the Surveyor's Guidelines for information on F691, F692, F693, F694, and F695

THE REGULATIONS

§483.25(f) Colostomy, urostomy, or ileostomy care.

The facility must ensure that residents who require colostomy, urostomy, or ileostomy services, receive such care consistent with professional standards of practice, the comprehensive person-centered care plan, and the resident's goals and preferences.

###

F692—Nutrition/Hydration Status Maintenance

See the Surveyor's Guidelines for information on F691, F692, F693, F694, and F695

THE REGULATIONS

§483.25(g) *Assisted nutrition and hydration.*

(Includes naso-gastric and gastrostomy tubes, both percutaneous endoscopic gastrostomy and percutaneous endoscopic jejunostomy, and enteral fluids). Based on *a resident's* comprehensive assessment, the facility must ensure that a resident—

§483.25(g)(1) Maintains acceptable parameters of nutritional status, such as *usual* body weight *or desirable body weight range* and *electrolyte balance*, unless the resident's clinical condition demonstrates that this is not possible *or resident preferences indicate otherwise;*

§483.25(g)*(2) Is offered* sufficient fluid intake to maintain proper hydration and health;

§483.25(g)(3) *Is offered* a therapeutic diet when there is a nutritional problem *and the health care provider orders a therapeutic diet.*

#

F693—Tube feeding Management/Restore

See the Surveyor's Guidelines for information on F691, F692, F693, F694, and F695

THE REGULATIONS

§483.25(g) *Assisted nutrition and hydration.*

(Includes naso-gastric and gastrostomy tubes, both percutaneous endoscopic gastrostomy and percutaneous endoscopic jejunostomy, and enteral fluids). Based on *a resident's* comprehensive assessment, the facility must ensure that a resident—

§483.25(g)(4)-(5) Enteral Nutrition

§483.25(g)*(4)* A resident who has been able to eat enough alone or with assistance is not fed by *enteral methods* unless the resident's clinical condition demonstrates that *enteral feeding was clinically indicated and consented to by the resident; and*

§483.25(g)*(5)* A resident who is fed *by enteral means* receives the appropriate treatment and services to *restore, if possible, oral eating skills and* to prevent *complications of enteral feeding including but not limited to* aspiration pneumonia, diarrhea, vomiting, dehydration, metabolic abnormalities, and nasal-pharyngeal ulcers.

F694—Parenteral/IV Fluids

See the Surveyor's Guidelines for information on F691, F692, F693, F694, and F695

THE REGULATIONS

§ 483.25(h) *Parenteral Fluids.*

Parenteral fluids must be administered consistent with professional standards of practice and in accordance with physician orders, the comprehensive person-centered care plan, and the resident's goals and preferences.

DEFINITION §483.25 (h)

Parenteral fluid

is defined as an IV infusion of various solutions to maintain adequate hydration, restore and/or maintain fluid volume, reestablish lost electrolytes, or provide partial nutrition which includes Total Parenteral Nutrition (TPN). Taken from http://medical-dictionary.thefreedictionary.com/administration+of+paren teral+fluids

###

F695—Respiratory/Tracheostomy Care and Suctioning

See the Surveyor's Guidelines for information on F691, F692, F693, F694, and F695

THE REGULATIONS

§483.25(i) Respiratory care, *including tracheostomy care and tracheal suctioning. The facility must ensure that a resident who needs respiratory care, including tracheostomy care and tracheal suctioning, is provided such care, consistent with professional standards of practice, the comprehensive person-centered care plan, the residents'* **goals and preferences, and 483.65 of this subpart.**

###

F696—Prostheses

See the Surveyor's Guidelines for information on F696.F697, F698, and F699.

THE REGULATIONS

§483.25(j) Prostheses

The facility must ensure that a resident who has a prosthesis is provided care and assistance, consistent with professional standards of practice, the comprehensive person-centered care plan, the residents' goals and preferences, to wear and be able to use the prosthetic device.

###

F697—Pain Management

See the Surveyor's Guidelines for information on F696.F697, F698, and F699.

THE REGULATIONS

§483.25(k) Pain Management.

The facility must ensure that pain management is provided to residents who require such services, consistent with professional standards of practice, the comprehensive person- centered care plan, and the residents' goals and preferences.

###

F698—Dialysis

See the Surveyor's Guidelines for information on F696.F697, F698, and F699.

THE REGULATIONS

§483.25(l) Dialysis.

The facility must ensure that residents who require dialysis receive such services, consistent with professional standards of practice, the comprehensive person-centered care plan, and the residents' goals and preferences

###

F699—(Phase 3) Trauma Informed Care

See the Surveyor's Guidelines for information on F696.F697, F698, and F699. Notice that this regulation and this F-Tag will not take effect until Phase 3.

THE REGULATIONS

§483.25(m) Trauma-informed care.

The facility must ensure that residents who are trauma survivors receive culturally competent, trauma-informed care in accordance with professional standards of practice and accounting for residents' experiences and preferences in order to eliminate or mitigate triggers that may cause re-traumatization of the resident.

[§483.25(m) will be implemented beginning November 28, 2019 (Phase 3)]

###

F700—Bedrails

THE REGULATIONS

§483.25(n) Bed Rails.

The facility must attempt to use appropriate alternatives prior to installing a side or bed rail. If a bed or side rail is used, the facility must ensure correct installation, use, and maintenance of bed rails, including but not limited to the following elements.

§483.25(n)(1) Assess the resident for risk of entrapment from bed rails prior to installation.

§483.25(n)(2) Review the risks and benefits of bed rails with the resident or resident representative and obtain informed consent prior to installation.

§483.25(n)(3) Ensure that the bed's dimensions are appropriate for the resident's size and weight.

§483.25(n)(4) Follow the manufacturers' recommendations and specifications for installing and maintaining bed rails.

DEFINITIONS

"Entrapment"

is an event in which a resident is caught, trapped, or entangled in the space in or about the bed rail.

"Bed rails"

are adjustable metal or rigid plastic bars that attach to the bed. They are available in a variety of types, shapes, and sizes ranging from full to one-half, one-quarter, or one-eighth lengths. Also, some bed rails are not designed as part of the bed by the manufacturer and may be installed on or used along the side of a bed

Examples of bed rails include, but are not limited to:

- *Side rails, bed side rails, and safety rails; and*

- *Grab bars and assist bars.*

INTENT

The intent of this requirement is to ensure that prior to the installation of bed rails, the facility has attempted to use alternatives; if the alternatives that were attempted were not adequate to meet the resident's needs, the resident is assessed for the use of bed rails, which includes a review of risks including entrapment; and informed consent is obtained from the resident or if applicable, the resident representative. The facility must ensure the bed is appropriate for the resident and that bed rails are properly installed and maintained

GUIDANCE: EXERPTS FROM THE SURVEYOR'S GUIDELINES

Even when bed rails are properly designed to reduce the risk of entrapment or falls, are compatible with the bed and mattress, and are used appropriately, they can present a hazard to certain individuals, particularly to people with physical limitations or altered mental status, such as dementia or delirium

See the Surveyor's Guidelines for additional information.

#

483.30 Physician Services

F-tags in this section include the following list. See the Surveyor's Guidelines for these regulations and the guidance associated with them.

F710—Resident's Care Supervised by a Physician

F711—Physician Visits—Review Care/Notes/Order

F712—Physician Visits-Frequency/Timelines/Alternate NPPs

F713—Physician for Emergency Care, Available 24 hours

F714—Physician Delegation of Tasks to NPP

F715—Physician Delegation to Dietitian/Therapist

483.35 Nursing Services

F725—Sufficient Nursing Staff

FOR VOICES FOR QUALITY CARE ADVOCATES

Note: Be aware that as of this writing, in Maryland the required direct care (nurses and aides combined) for each resident in each 24 hour period is just <u>2.0 hours</u>. That number in Washington is <u>4.1 hours</u> of direct care for each resident in each 24 hour period.

FROM THE DISTRICT OF COLUMBIA REGULATIONS: Beginning January 1, 2012, each facility shall provide a minimum daily average of four and one tenth (4.1) hours of direct nursing care per resident per day, of which at least six tenths (0.6) hours shall be provided by an advanced practice registered nurse or registered nurse, which shall be in addition to any coverage required by subsection 3211.4.

THE REGULATIONS

§483.35 Nursing Services

The facility must have sufficient nursing staff *with the appropriate competencies and skills set*s to provide nursing and related services to *assure resident safety and* attain or maintain the highest practicable physical, mental, and psychosocial well-being of each resident, as determined by resident assessments and individual plans of care *and considering the number, acuity and diagnoses of the facility's resident population in accordance with the facility assessment required at §483.70(e).*

§483.35(a) Sufficient Staff.

§483.**35**(a)(1) The facility must provide services by sufficient numbers of each of the following types of personnel on a 24-hour basis to provide nursing care to all residents in accordance with resident care plans:

- (i) Except when waived under paragraph (e) of this section, licensed nurses; and
- (ii) Other nursing personnel, *including but not limited to nurse aides.*

§483.**35**(a)(2) Except when waived under paragraph (*e*) of this section, the facility must designate a licensed nurse to serve as a charge nurse on each tour of duty.

DEFINITIONS

"Nurse Aide"

> as defined in §483.5, is any individual providing nursing or nursing-related services to residents in a facility. This term may also include an individual who provides these services through an agency or under a contract with the facility, but is not a licensed health professional, a registered dietitian, or someone who volunteers to provide such services without pay. Nurse aides do not include those individuals who furnish services to residents only as paid feeding assistants as defined in §488.301.

###

F726—Competent Nursing Staff

THE REGULATIONS

§483.35 Nursing Services

The facility must have sufficient nursing staff *with the appropriate competencies and skills sets* to provide nursing and related services to *assure resident safety and* attain or maintain the highest practicable physical, mental, and psychosocial well-being of each resident, as determined by resident assessments and individual plans of care *and considering the number, acuity and diagnoses of the facility's resident population in accordance with the facility assessment required at §483.70(e).*

§483.35(a)*(3) The facility must ensure that licensed nurses have the specific competencies and skill sets necessary to care for residents' needs, as identified through resident assessments, and described in the plan of care.*

§483.35(a)*(4) Providing care includes but is not limited to assessing, evaluating, planning and implementing resident care plans and responding to resident's needs.*

§483.35*(c)* Proficiency of nurse aides.

The facility must ensure that nurse aides are able to demonstrate competency in skills and techniques necessary to care for residents' needs, as identified through resident assessments, and described in the plan of care.

DEFINITIONS

"Competency"

is a measurable pattern of knowledge, skills, abilities, behaviors, and other characteristics that an individual needs to perform work roles or occupational functions successfully.

GUIDANCE: EXERPTS FROM THE SURVEYOR'S GUIDELINES

Cultural Competencies

Cultural competencies help staff communicate effectively with residents and their families and help provide care that is appropriate to the culture and the individual. The term cultural competence (also known as cultural responsiveness, cultural awareness, and cultural sensitivity) refers to a person's ability to interact effectively with persons of cultures different from his/her own. With regard to health care, cultural competence is a set of behaviors and attitudes held by clinicians that allows them to communicate effectively with individuals of various cultural backgrounds and to plan for and provide care that is appropriate to the culture and to the individual.

###

F727—RN 8 Hrs/7 days/Wk. Full Time DON

FOR VOICES FOR QUALITY CARE ADVOCATES

This, basically, is all there is in the federal regulations regarding staffing in nursing homes other than the requirement that facilities have "sufficient staff" to care for the residents. In any situation where the level of staffing is involved, an advocate should look to State laws and regulations rather than relying on these federal regulations.

THE REGULATIONS

§483.35(b) Registered nurse

§483.35(b)(1) Except when waived under paragraph *(e)* or *(f)* of this section, the facility must use the services of a registered nurse for at least 8 consecutive hours a day, 7 days a week.

§483.35(b)(2) Except when waived under paragraph *(e)* or *(f)* of this section, the facility must designate a registered nurse to serve as the director of nursing on a full time basis.

§483.35(b)(3) The director of nursing may serve as a charge nurse only when the facility has an average daily occupancy of 60 or fewer residents.

DEFINITIONS

"Full-time"

is defined as working 35 or more hours a week.

GUIDANCE: EXERPTS FROM THE SURVEYOR'S GUIDELINES

The facility **must** designate a registered nurse (RN) to serve as the DON on a full-time basis. The facility can only be waived from this requirement if it has a waiver under subsection

§§483.35 (e) or **(f).** This requirement can be met when **two or more** RNs share the **DON** position. **The roles and responsibilities for each individual serving as the DON must be clearly defined and all** facility staff must understand **how these responsibilities are** shared **among the individuals functioning as the DON.**

###

F728—Facility Hiring and Use of Nurse

THE REGULATIONS

§483.35(d) Requirement for facility hiring and use of nurse aides-

§483.*35(d)(1)* General rule.

A facility must not use any individual working in the facility as a nurse aide for more than 4 months, on a full-time basis, unless—

- (i) That individual is competent to provide nursing and nursing related services; and
- (ii)(A) That individual has completed a training and competency evaluation program, or a competency evaluation program approved by the State as meeting the requirements of §483.151 through §483.154; or
    - ○ (B) That individual has been deemed or determined competent as provided in §483.150(a) and (b).

§483.*35(d)(2)* Non-permanent employees.

A facility must not use on a temporary, per diem, leased, or any basis other than a permanent employee any individual who does not meet the requirements in paragraphs (d)(1)(i) and (ii) of this section.

§483.*35(d)(3) Minimum* Competency

A facility must not use any individual who has worked less than 4 months as a nurse aide in that facility unless the individual—

- (i) Is a full-time employee in a State-approved training and competency evaluation program;
- (ii) Has demonstrated competence through satisfactory participation in a State- approved nurse aide training and competency evaluation program or competency evaluation program; or
- (iii) Has been deemed or determined competent as provided in §483.150(a) and (b).

DEFINITIONS

A **"permanent employee"** is defined as any employee the facility expects to continue working on an ongoing basis.

GUIDANCE: EXERPTS FROM THE SURVEYOR'S GUIDELINES

Any individual who successfully completed *either a nurse aide training or* competency evaluation program *(NATCEP)* or a competency evaluation program *(CEP) or* has been deemed or determined competent as provided in §483.150(a) and (b) *may be employed as a nurse aide.*

If an individual has not *successfully* completed a *NATCEP* program at the time of employment, that individual *may only function* as a nurse aide if the individual is *currently* in a *NATCE*P (**not a competency evaluation program (CEP) alone**) *and* is a permanent employee in his or her first four months of employment in the facility.

#

F729—Nurse Aide Registry Verfication, Retraining

THE REGULATIONS

§483.35(d)(4) Registry verification.

Before allowing an individual to serve as a nurse aide, a facility must receive registry verification that the individual has met competency evaluation requirements unless—

- (i) The individual is a full-time employee in a training and competency evaluation program approved by the State; or
- (ii) The individual can prove that he or she has recently successfully completed a training and competency evaluation program or competency evaluation program approved by the State and has not yet been included in the registry. Facilities must follow up to ensure that such an individual actually becomes registered.

§483.35(d)(5) Multi-State registry verification.

Before allowing an individual to serve as a nurse aide, a facility must seek information from every State registry established under sections 1819(e)(2)(A) or 1919(e)(2)(A) of the Act *that* the facility believes will include information on the individual.

§483.35(d)(6) Required retraining.

If, since an individual's most recent completion of a training and competency evaluation program, there has been a continuous period of 24 consecutive months during none of which the individual provided nursing or nursing-related services for monetary compensation, the individual must complete a new training and competency evaluation program or a new competency evaluation program.

GUIDANCE: EXERPTS FROM THE SURVEYOR'S GUIDELINES

If the **nurse aide provides documentation to verify that** he or she performed nursing or nursing- related services for monetary compensation **(including providing assistance with activities of daily living (ADL) care)** for at least one documented day (e.g., 8 consecutive hours) during the previous 24 months, **he/she is not required to take a new nurse aide training and competency evaluation program or a new competency evaluation program (NATCEP/CEP). It is not required that these services be provided in a nursing home setting so long as the nurse aide was performing nursing or nursing-related services including assisting with ADLs.** The State is required to remove the individual's name from the registry if the services are not provided for monetary compensation during the 24-month period.

###

F730—Nurse Aide Perform Review—12 Hr/Year inservice

THE REGULATIONS

§483.*35(d)(7)* Regular in-service education.

The facility must complete a performance review of every nurse aide at least once every 12 months, and must provide regular in-service education based on the outcome of these reviews. ***In-service training must comply with the requirements of §483.95(g).***

###

F731—Waiver—Licensed Nurses 24Hr/Day and RN Coverage

See the Surveyor's Guidelines for information on this F-Tag.

https://www.cms.gov/Medicare/Provider-Enrollment-and-Certification/GuidanceforLawsAndRegulations/Downloads/Advance-Appendix-PP-Including-Phase-2-.pdf

###

F732—Posted Nurse Staffing Information

FOR VOICES FOR QUALITY CARE ADVOCATES

The regulations in this F-Tag are very important. This regulation is the basis of the right to know at any given time exactly who is responsible for direct care. Some states have additional requirements for these posting regulations.

THE REGULATIONS

§483.35*(g)* Nurse Staffing Information.

§483.35*(g)*(1) Data requirements. The facility must post the following information on a daily basis:

- (i) Facility name.
- (ii) The current date.
- (iii) The total number and the actual hours worked by the following categories of licensed and unlicensed nursing staff directly responsible for resident care per shift:
  - (A) Registered nurses.
  - (B) Licensed practical nurses or licensed vocational nurses (as defined under State law).
  - (C) Certified nurse aides.
- (iv) Resident census.

§483.35*(g)*(2) Posting requirements.

- (i) The facility must post the nurse staffing data specified in paragraph *(g)*(1) of this section on a daily basis at the beginning of each shift.
- (ii) Data must be posted as follows:
  - (A) Clear and readable format.
  - (B) In a prominent place readily accessible to residents and visitors.

§483.35*(g)(3)* Public access to posted nurse staffing data. The facility must, upon oral or written request, make nurse staffing data available to the public for review at a cost not to exceed the community standard.

§483.35*(g)*(4) Facility data retention requirements. The facility must maintain the posted daily nurse staffing data for a minimum of 18 months, or as required by State law, whichever is greater.

INTENT

To make staffing information readily available in a readable format to residents and visitors at any given time.

GUIDANCE: EXERPTS FROM THE SURVEYOR'S GUIDELINES

The facility's "document" may be a form or spreadsheet, as long as all the required information is displayed clearly and in a visible place. The information should be displayed in a prominent place accessible to residents and visitors and presented in a clear and readable format. This information posted must be up-to-date and current.

The facility is required to list the total number of staff and the actual hours worked by the staff to meet this regulatory requirement. The information should reflect staff absences on that shift due to call-outs and illness.

Staffing must include all nursing staff who are paid by the facility (including contract staff). The nursing home would not include in the posting staff paid for through other sources; examples include hospice staff covered by the hospice benefit, or individuals hired by families to provide companionship or assistance to a specific resident.

###

483.40 Behavioral Health Services

For guidance under the F-Tags in this section, see the Surveyor's Guidelines.

https://www.cms.gov/Medicare/Provider-Enrollment-and-Certification/GuidanceforLawsAndRegulations/Downloads/Advance-Appendix-PP-Including-Phase-2-.pdf

#

F740—Behavioral Health Services

FOR VOICES FOR QUALITY CARE ADVOCATES

The regulations under this F-Tag are included in the temporary moratorium on full enforcement.

THE REGULATIONS

§483.40 Behavioral health services.

Each resident must receive and the facility must provide the necessary behavioral health care and services to attain or maintain the highest practicable physical, mental, and psychosocial well-being, in accordance with the comprehensive assessment and plan of care. Behavioral health encompasses a resident's whole emotional and mental well-being, which includes, but is not limited to, the prevention and treatment of mental and substance use disorders.

#

F741—Sufficient/Competent Staff—Behav Health Needs

FOR VOICES FOR QUALITY CARE ADVOCATES

The regulations under this F-Tag are included in the temporary moratorium on full enforcement.

THE REGULATIONS

§483.40(a) The facility must have sufficient staff who provide direct services to residents with the appropriate competencies and skills sets to provide nursing and related services to assure resident safety and attain or maintain the highest practicable physical, mental and psychosocial well-being of each resident, as determined by resident assessments and individual plans of care and considering the number, acuity and diagnoses of the facility's resident population in accordance with §483.70(e). These competencies and skills sets include, but are not limited to, knowledge of and appropriate training and supervision for:

§483.40(a)(1) Caring for residents with mental and psychosocial disorders, as well as residents with a history of trauma and/or post-traumatic stress disorder, that have been identified in the facility assessment conducted pursuant to

§483.70(e), and as linked to history of trauma and/or post-traumatic stress disorder, will be implemented beginning November 28, 2019 (Phase 3).

§483.40(a)(2) Implementing non-pharmacological interventions

###

F742—Treatment/Svc for Mental/Psychosocial Concerns

THE REGULATIONS

§483.*40(b)* Based on the comprehensive assessment of a resident, the facility must ensure that—

§483.*40(b)*(1)

A resident who displays *or is diagnosed with* mental **disorder** or psychosocial adjustment difficulty, **or who has a history of trauma and/or post-traumatic stress disorder,** receives appropriate treatment and services to correct the assessed problem **or to attain the highest practicable mental and psychosocial well-being;**

###

F743—No Pattern of Behavioral Difficulties Unless Unavoidable

THE REGULATIONS

§483.*40*(b)(2) A resident whose assessment did not reveal **or who does not have a diagnosis of** a mental or psychosocial adjustment difficulty **or a documented history of trauma and/or post-traumatic stress disorder** does not display a pattern of decreased social interaction and/or increased withdrawn, angry, or depressive behaviors, unless the resident's clinical condition demonstrates that development of such a pattern was unavoidable; **and**

###

F744—Treatment/Service for Dementia

THE REGULATIONS

§483.40(b)(3) A resident who displays or is diagnosed with dementia, receives the appropriate treatment and services to attain or maintain his or her highest practicable physical, mental, and psychosocial well-being.

###

F745—Provision of Medically Related Social Services

THE REGULATIONS

§483.*40(d)* The facility must provide medically-related social services to attain or maintain the highest practicable physical, mental and psychosocial well-being of each resident.

###

483.45 Pharmacy Services

See the Surveyor's Guidelines for information on this F-Tag.

https://www.cms.gov/Medicare/Provider-Enrollment-and-Certification/GuidanceforLawsAndRegulations/Downloads/Advance-Appendix-PP-Including-Phase-2-.pdf

F755—Pharmacy Svcs/Procedures/Pharmacist/Records

THE REGULATIONS

§483.**45** Pharmacy Services

The facility must provide routine and emergency drugs and biologicals to its residents, or obtain them under an agreement described in §483.**70(g)**. The facility may permit unlicensed personnel to administer drugs if State law permits, but only under the general supervision of a licensed nurse.

§483.**45**(a) Procedures. A facility must provide pharmaceutical services (including procedures that assure the accurate acquiring, receiving, dispensing, and administering of all drugs and biologicals) to meet the needs of each resident.

§483.**45**(b) Service Consultation. The facility must employ or obtain the services of a licensed pharmacist who—

§483.**45**(b)(1) Provides consultation on all aspects of the provision of pharmacy services in the facility.

§483.**45(b)(2) Establishes a system of records of receipt and disposition of all controlled drugs in sufficient detail to enable an accurate reconciliation; and**

§483.**45(b)(3) Determines that drug records are in order and that an account of all controlled drugs is maintained and periodically reconciled.**

DEFINITIONS §483.45

Definitions are provided to clarify terminology related to pharmaceutical services and the management of each resident's medication regimen for effectiveness and safety.

"Acquiring medication"

is the process by which a facility requests and obtains a medication.

"Biologicals"

are made from a variety of natural sources—human, animal, or microorganisms. Biologicals are used to treat, prevent, or diagnose diseases and medical conditions. They may include a wide range of products such as vaccines, blood and blood components, allergenics, somatic cells, gene therapy, tissues, and recombinant therapeutic proteins.

"Controlled Medications"

are substances that have an accepted medical use (medications which fall under US Drug Enforcement Agency (DEA) Schedules II—V), have a potential for abuse, ranging from low to high, and may also lead to physical or psychological dependence.

Dispensing"

is a process that includes the interpretation of a prescription; selection, measurement, and packaging or repackaging of the product (as necessary); and labeling of the medication or device pursuant to a prescription/order.

"Disposition"

is the process of returning and/or destroying unused medications

"Diversion of medications"

is the transfer of a controlled substance or other medication from a lawful to an unlawful channel of distribution or use, as adapted from the Uniform Controlled Substances Act.

"Pharmaceutical Services" refers to:

The process (including documentation, as applicable) of receiving and interpreting prescriber's orders; acquiring, receiving, storing, controlling, reconciling, compounding (e.g., intravenous antibiotics), dispensing, packaging, labeling, distributing, administering, monitoring responses to, using and/or disposing of all medications, biologicals, chemicals (e.g., povidone iodine, hydrogen peroxide);

The provision of medication-related information to health care professionals and residents;

The process of identifying, evaluating and addressing medication-related issues including the prevention and reporting of medication errors; and

The provision, monitoring and/or the use of medication-related devices.

"Pharmacy assistant or technician"

refers to the ancillary personnel who work under the supervision and delegation of the pharmacist, consistent with state requirements.

"Receiving medication"—

for the purpose of this guidance—is the process that a facility uses to ensure that medications, accepted from the facility's pharmacy or an outside source (e.g., vending pharmacy delivery agent, Veterans Administration, family member), are accurate (e.g., doses, amount).

"Reconciliation"—

for the purpose of this guidance—refers to a system of recordkeeping that ensures an accurate inventory of medications by accounting for controlled medications that have been received, dispensed, administered, and/or, including the process of disposition

###

F756—Drug Regimen Review, Report Irregular, Act On

THE REGULATIONS

§483.45(c) Drug Regimen Review.

§483.45(c)(1) The drug regimen of each resident must be reviewed at least once a month by a licensed pharmacist.

§483.45(c)(2) This review must include a review of the resident's medical chart.

§483.45(c)*(4)* The pharmacist must report any irregularities to the attending physician *and the facility's medical director* and director of nursing, and these reports must be acted upon.

- *(i) Irregularities include, but are not limited to, any drug that meets the criteria set forth in paragraph (d) of this section for an unnecessary drug.*
- *(ii) Any irregularities noted by the pharmacist during this review must be documented on a separate, written report that is sent to the attending physician and the facility's medical director and director of nursing and lists, at a minimum, the resident's name, the relevant drug, and the irregularity the pharmacist identified.*
- *(iii) The attending physician must document in the resident's medical record that the identified irregularity has been reviewed and what, if any, action has been taken to address it. If there is to be no change in the medication, the attending physician should document his or her rationale in the resident's medical record.*

§483.45(c)*(5) The facility must develop and maintain policies and procedures for the monthly drug regimen review that include, but are not limited to, time frames for the different steps in the process and steps the pharmacist must take when he or she identifies an irregularity that requires urgent action to protect the resident.*

F757—Drug Regimen is Free From Unnecessary Drugs

THE REGULATIONS

§483.*45(d)* Unnecessary Drugs—General.

Each resident's drug regimen must be free from unnecessary drugs. An unnecessary drug is any drug when used—

§483.*45(d)(1)* In excessive dose (including duplicate *drug* therapy); or

§483.*45(d)(2)* For excessive duration; or

§483.45(d)(3) Without adequate monitoring; or

§483.45(d)(4) Without adequate indications for its use; or

§483.*45(d)(5)* In the presence of adverse consequences which indicate the dose should be reduced or discontinued; or

§483.*45(d)(6)* Any combinations of the reasons stated *in paragraphs (d)(1) through (5) of this section.*

###

F758—Free from Unnecessary Psychotropic Meds/PRN Use

FOR VOICES FOR QUALITY CARE ADVOCATES

The regulations under this F-Tag are included in the temporary moratorium on full enforcement.

THE REGULATIONS

§483.*45*(c)*(3) A psychotropic drug is any drug that affects brain activities associated with mental processes and behavior. These drugs include, but are not limited to, drugs in the following categories:*

- *(i) Anti-psychotic;*
- *(ii) Anti-depressant;*
- *(iii) Anti-anxiety; and*
- *(iv) Hypnotic*

§483.*45(e) Psychotropic* Drugs. Based on a comprehensive assessment of a resident, the facility must ensure that--

§483.*45(e)(1)* Residents who have not used p*sychotropic* drugs are not given these drugs unless the medication is necessary to treat a specific condition as diagnosed and documented in the clinical record;

§483.*45(e)(2)* Residents who use *psychotropic* drugs receive gradual dose reductions, and behavioral interventions, unless clinically contraindicated, in an effort to discontinue these drugs;

§483.*45(e)(3) Residents do not receive psychotropic drugs pursuant to a PRN order unless that medication is necessary to treat a diagnosed specific condition that is documented in the clinical record; and*

§483.*45(e)(4) PRN orders for psychotropic drugs are limited to 14 days. Except as provided in*

248

§483.*45(e)(5), if the attending physician or prescribing practitioner believes that it is appropriate for the PRN order to be extended beyond 14 days, he or she should document their rationale in the resident's medical record and indicate the duration for the PRN order.*

§483.*45(e)(5) PRN orders for anti-psychotic drugs are limited to 14 days and cannot be renewed unless the attending physician or prescribing practitioner evaluates the resident for the appropriateness of that medication.*

###

F759—Free of Medication Error Rates of 5% or More

THE REGULATIONS

§483.**45(f)** Medication Errors. The facility must ensure that its—

§483.**45(f)(1)** Medication error rates are not 5 percent or greater; and

#

F760—Residents Are Free of Significant Med Errors

FOR VOICES FOR QUALITY CARE ADVOCATES

We have been called in to assist in a number of cases where medication errors and improperly prescribed medications have caused not only unpleasant side effects but also serious harm. For instances where medicine errors are suspected, review the records including the doctor's orders and the medicine and daily treatment charts.

THE REGULATIONS

The facility must ensure that *its*—

§483.**45(f)(2)** Residents are free of any significant medication errors.

DEFINITIONS

"Medication Error"

*means the observed **or identified** preparation or administration of medications or biologicals which is not in accordance with:*

- *1. The prescriber's order;*

- *2. Manufacturer's specifications (not recommendations) regarding the preparation and administration of the medication or biological; or*

- *3. Accepted professional standards and principles which apply to professionals providing services. Accepted professional standards and principles include the various practice regulations in each State, and current commonly accepted health standards established by national organizations, boards, and councils.*

"Significant medication error"

*means one which causes the resident discomfort or jeopardizes his or her health and safety. Criteria for judging significant medication errors as well as examples are provided **below. Significance** may be subjective or relative depending on the individual situation **and duration**, e.g., constipation that is unrelieved **because an ordered** laxative **is omitted for one day**, resulting in a medication error, may **cause a resident** slight discomfort or perhaps no discomfort at all. **However, if this omission leads to** constipation **that** persists for greater than three days, the **medication error** may be **deemed** significant **since** constipation **that** causes an obstruction or fecal impaction can **directly** jeopardize the resident's health and safety.*

"Medication error rate"

is determined by calculating the percentage of medication errors observed during a medication administration observation. The numerator in the ratio is the total number of errors that the survey team observes, both significant and non-significant. The denominator consists of the total number of observations or "opportunities for errors" and includes all the doses the survey team observed being administered plus the doses ordered but not administered. The equation for calculating a medication error rate is as follows:

Medication Error Rate   =   Number of Errors Observed divided by the Opportunities for Errors (doses given plus doses ordered but not given) X 100.

The error rate must be 5% or greater in order to cite F759. Rounding up of a lower rate (e.g., 4.6%) to a 5% rate is not permitted. A medication error rate of 5% or greater may indicate that systemic problems exist. The survey team should consider investigating additional potential noncompliance issues, such as F755– Pharmacy Services, related to the facility's medication distribution system

# # #

F761—Label/Store Drugs & Biologicals

THE REGULATIONS

§483.*45(g)* Labeling of Drugs and Biologicals

Drugs and biologicals used in the facility must be labeled in accordance with currently accepted professional principles, and include the appropriate accessory and cautionary instructions, and the expiration date when applicable.

§483.*45(h)* Storage of Drugs and Biologicals

§483.*45(h)*(1) In accordance with State and Federal laws, the facility must store all drugs and biologicals in locked compartments under proper temperature controls, and permit only authorized personnel to have access to the keys.

§483.*45(h)*(2) The facility must provide separately locked, permanently affixed compartments for storage of controlled drugs listed in Schedule II of the Comprehensive Drug Abuse Prevention and Control Act of 1976 and other drugs subject to abuse, except when the facility uses single unit package drug distribution systems in which the quantity stored is minimal and a missing dose can be readily detected.

DEFINITIONS

Biologicals"

are made from a variety of natural sources—human, animal, or microorganisms. Biologics are used to treat, prevent, or diagnose diseases and medical conditions. They may include a wide range of products such as vaccines, blood and blood components, allergenics, somatic cells, gene therapy, tissues, and recombinant therapeutic proteins.

"Controlled Medications"

are substances that have an accepted medical use (medications which fall under US Drug Enforcement Agency (DEA) Schedules II—V), have a potential for abuse, ranging from low to high, and may also lead to physical or psychological dependence.

#

483.50 Laboratory, Radiology, and Other Diagnostic Services

See the Surveyor's Guidelines for information on this F-Tag.

https://www.cms.gov/Medicare/Provider-Enrollment-and-Certification/GuidanceforLawsAndRegulations/Downloads/Advance-Appendix-PP-Including-Phase-2-.pdf

F770—Laboratory Services

F771—Blood Bank and Transfusion Services

F772—Lab Services Not Provided On-Site

F773—Lab Svs Physician Order/Notify of Results

F774—Assist with Transport Arrangements to Lab Svcs

F775—Lab Reports In Record—Lab Name/Address

F776—Radiology/Other Diagnostic Services

F777—Radiology/Diagnosis Svs Ordered/Notify Results

F778—Assist with Transport Arrangements to Radiology

F779—X-Ray/Diagnostic Report in Record—Sign/Dated

###

483.55 Dental Services

F790—Routine/Emergency Dental Services in SNFs

FOR VOICES FOR QUALITY CARE ADVOCATES

This is another area where Maryland falls behind the curve. The Maryland State Manual, as of this writing, does not provide for Routine Dental Care for people in Nursing Homes who are receiving Medicaid Funding. **HOWEVER, Maryland Medicaid will allow payments for insurance which includes Dental Insurance to be paid out of any income that resident may have under Other Medical Expenses.** Voices recommends that anyone living in a nursing home who needs routine dental care purchase dental insurance to cover these bills and declare it on the Medicaid applications.

See the Intent, Definitions, and Guidance under F791.

THE REGULATIONS

§483.55 Dental services.

The facility must assist residents in obtaining routine and 24-hour emergency dental care.

§483.55(a) Skilled Nursing Facilities A facility—

§483.55(a)(1) Must provide or obtain from an outside resource, in accordance with with §483.*70(g)* of this part, routine and emergency dental services to meet the needs of each resident;

§483.55(a)(2) May charge a Medicare resident an additional amount for routine and emergency dental services;

§483.55(a)(3) Must have a policy identifying those circumstances when the loss or damage of dentures is the facility's responsibility and may not charge a resident for the loss or damage of dentures determined in accordance with facility policy to be the facility's responsibility;

§483.55(a)(4) Must if necessary *or if requested*, assist the resident;

- (i) In making appointments; and
- *(ii)* By arranging for transportation to and from *the dental services location; and*

§483.55(a)(5) Must promptly, within 3 days, refer residents with lost or damaged dentures for dental services. If a referral does not occur within 3 days, the facility must provide documentation of what they did to ensure the resident could still eat and drink adequately while awaiting dental services and the extenuating circumstances that led to the delay.

#

F791—Routine/Emergency Dental Services in NFs

FOR VOICES FOR QUALITY CARE ADVOCATES

See F90 above for suggested procedures for people living in Maryland nursing homes.

THE REGULATIONS

§483.55 Dental Services

The facility must assist residents in obtaining routine and 24-hour emergency dental care.

§483.55(b) Nursing Facilities. The facility—

§483.55(b)(1) Must provide or obtain from an outside resource, in accordance with *§483.70(g)* of this part, the following dental services to meet the needs of each resident:

- (i) Routine dental services (to the extent covered under the State plan); and
- *(ii)* Emergency dental services;

§483.55(b)(2) Must, if necessary *or if requested,* assist the resident—

- (i) In making appointments; and
- (ii) By arranging for transportation to and from *the dental services locations;*

§483.55(b)(3) Must *promptly, within 3 days,* refer residents with lost or damaged dentures *for dental services. If a referral does not occur within 3 days, the facility must provide documentation of what they did to ensure the resident could still eat and drink adequately while awaiting dental services and the extenuating circumstances that led to the delay;*

§483.55(b)(4) Must have a policy identifying those circumstances when the loss or damage of dentures is the facility's responsibility and may not charge a resident for the loss or damage of dentures determined in accordance with facility policy to be the facility's responsibility; and

§483.55(b)(5) Must assist residents who are eligible and wish to participate to apply for reimbursement of dental services as an incurred medical expense under the State plan

DEFINITIONS

"Emergency dental services"

includes services needed to treat an episode of acute pain in teeth, gums, or palate; broken, or otherwise damaged teeth, or any other problem of the oral cavity that required immediate attention by a dentist.

"Promptly"

means within 3 business days or less from the time the loss or damage to dentures is identified unless the facility can provide documentation of extenuating circumstances that resulted in the delay.

"Routine dental services"

means an annual inspection of the oral cavity for signs of disease, diagnosis of dental disease, dental radiographs as needed, dental cleaning, fillings (new and repairs), minor partial or full denture adjustments, smoothing of broken teeth, and limited prosthodontic procedures, e.g., taking impressions for dentures and fitting dentures.

INTENT of §§483.55(a)[F790] & (b) [F791]

To ensure that residents obtain needed dental services, including routine dental services; *to ensure the* facility *provides the assistance needed or requested to obtain these services; to ensure the resident is not inappropriately charged for these services; and if a referral does not occur within three business days, documentation of the facility's to ensure the resident could still eat and drink adequately while awaiting dental services and the extenuating circumstances that led to the delay.*

GUIDANCE: EXERPTS FROM THE SURVEYOR'S GUIDELINES §483.55(a)[F790] & (b) [F791]

A dentist **must be** available for each resident. The dentist can be directly employed by the facility or the facility can have a written contractual agreement with a dentist. The facility may also choose to have a written agreement for dentist services from a dental clinic, dental school or a dental hygienist all of whom are working within Federal and State laws and under the direct supervision of a dentist.

For Medicare and private pay residents, facilities are responsible for having the services available, but may bill an additional charge for the services.

For Medicaid residents, the facility must provide all emergency dental services and those routine dental services to the extent covered under the Medicaid state plan. The facility must inform the resident of the deduction for the incurred medical expense available under the Medicaid state plan and must assist the resident in applying for the deduction.

See the Surveyor's Guidelines for additional information.

https://www.cms.gov/Medicare/Provider-Enrollment-and-Certification/GuidanceforLawsAndRegulations/Downloads/Advance-Appendix-PP-Including-Phase-2-.pdf

#

483.60 Food and Nutrition Services

F800—Provided Diet Meets Needs of Each Resident

THE REGULATIONS

§483.60 *Food and nutrition services.*

The facility must provide each resident with a nourishing, palatable, well-balanced diet that meets *his or her* daily nutritional and special dietary needs, *taking into consideration the preferences of each resident.*

GUIDANCE: EXERPTS FROM THE SURVEYOR'S GUIDELINES

This requirement *expects that there is ongoing* communication and *coordination among and* between staff within all departments to ensure that the resident assessment, care plan and actual food *and nutrition* services meet *each resident's* daily nutritional and dietary needs and choices.

While it may be challenging to meet every residents' individual preferences, incorporating a residents' preferences and *dietary* needs will ensure residents are offered meaningful choices in *meals*/diets that are nutritionally adequate and satisfying to the individual. *Reasonable efforts to accommodate these choices and preferences must be addressed by facility staff.*

###

F801—Qualified Dietary Staff

THE REGULATIONS

§483.60(a) Staffing

The facility must employ *sufficient staff with the appropriate competencies and skills sets to carry out the functions of the food and nutrition service, taking into consideration resident assessments, individual plans of care and the number, acuity and diagnoses of the facility's resident population in accordance with the facility assessment required at §483.70(e)*

This includes:

§483.60(a)(1) A qualified dietitian *or other clinically qualified nutrition professional* either full-time, part-time, or on a consultant basis. A qualified dietitian *or other clinically qualified nutrition professional* is one who—

- *(i) Holds a bachelor's or higher degree granted by a regionally accredited college or university in the United States (or an equivalent foreign degree) with completion of the academic requirements of a program in nutrition or dietetics accredited by an appropriate national accreditation organization recognized for this purpose.*
- *(ii) Has completed at least 900 hours of supervised dietetics practice under the supervision of a registered dietitian or nutrition professional.*
- *(iii) Is licensed or certified as a dietitian or nutrition professional by the State in which the services are performed. In a State that does not provide for licensure or certification, the individual will be deemed to have met this requirement if he or she is recognized as a "registered dietitian" by the Commission on Dietetic Registration or its successor organization, or meets the*

requirements of paragraphs (a)(1)(i) and (ii) of this section.

- *(iv) For dietitians hired or contracted with prior to November 28, 2016, meets these requirements no later than 5 years after November 28, 2016 or as required by state law.*

§483.**60**(a)(2) If a qualified dietitian *or other clinically qualified nutrition professional* is not employed full-time, the facility must designate a person to serve as the director of food *and nutrition* services *who—*

- *(i) For designations prior to November 28, 2016, meets the following requirements no later than 5 years after November 28, 2016, or no later than 1 year after November 28, 2016 for designations after November 28, 2016, is:*
  - ○ *(A) A certified dietary manager; or*
  - ○ *(B) A certified food service manager; or*
  - ○ *(C) Has similar national certification for food service management and safety from a national certifying body; or*
  - ○ *(D) Has an associate's or higher degree in food service management or in hospitality, if the course study includes food service or restaurant management, from an accredited institution of higher learning; and*
- *(ii) In States that have established standards for food service managers or dietary managers, meets State requirements for food service managers or dietary managers, and*
- *(iii)* Receives frequently scheduled consultations from a qualified dietitian *or other clinically qualified nutrition professional.*

DEFINITIONS

"Full-time"

means working 35 or more hours a week.

"Part-time"

employees typically work fewer hours in a day or during a work week than full-time employees. The U.S. Department of Labor, Bureau of Statistics uses a definition of 34 or fewer hours a week as part-time work. Part-time workers may also be those who only work during certain parts of the year.

"Consultants"

means an individual who gives professional advice or services. They are generally not direct employees of the facility and may work either full or part-time.

###

F802—Sufficient Dietary Support Personnel

THE REGULATIONS

§483.**60**(a) Staffing

The facility must employ **sufficient staff with the appropriate competencies and skills sets to carry out the functions of the food and nutrition service, taking into consideration resident assessments, individual plans of care and the number, acuity and diagnoses of the facility's resident population in accordance with the facility assessment required at §483.70(e).**

§483.60(a)(3) Support staff.

The facility must provide sufficient support personnel **to safely and effectively** carry out the functions of the **food and nutrition** service.

§483.60(b) A member of the Food and Nutrition Services staff must participate on the interdisciplinary team as required in § 483.21(b)(2)(ii).

DEFINITIONS

"Sufficient support personnel"

means having enough *dietary and food and nutrition* staff to *safely carry out all of the functions of the food and nutrition services. This does not include staff, such as licensed nurses, nurse aides or paid feeding assistants, involved in assisting residents with eating.*

#

F803—Menus Meet Res Needs/Prep in Advance/Followed

THE REGULATIONS

§483.60(c) Menus and nutritional adequacy. Menus must-

§483.60(c)(1) Meet the nutritional needs of residents in accordance with **established national guidelines.;**

§483.60(c)(2) Be prepared in advance;

§483.60(c)(3) Be followed;

§483.60(c)(4) Reflect, based on a facility's reasonable efforts, the religious, cultural and ethnic needs of the resident population, as well as input received from residents and resident groups;

§483.60(c)(5) Be updated periodically;

§483.60(c)(6) Be reviewed by the facility's dietitian or other clinically qualified nutrition professional for nutritional adequacy; and

§483.60(c)(7) Nothing in this paragraph should be construed to limit the resident's right to make personal dietary choices.

DEFINITIONS

"Reasonable effort"

means assessing individual resident needs and preferences and demonstrating actions to meet those needs and preferences, including reviewing availability procurement sources of such food items, identifying preparation methods and approaches, and determining whether purchasing and serving such items can occur.

"Periodically"

means that a facility should update its menus to accommodate their changing resident population or resident needs as determined by their facility assessment. See F838. This includes ethnic, cultural, or religious factors that may potentially affect the care provided by the facility, including, but not limited to, activities and food and nutrition services.

GUIDANCE: EXERPTS FROM THE SURVEYOR'S GUIDELINES

The facility must make reasonable efforts to provide food that is appetizing to and culturally appropriate for residents. This means learning the resident's needs and preferences and responding to them. For residents with dementia or other barriers or challenges to expressing their preferences, facility staff should document the steps taken to learn what those preferences are.

It is not required that there be individualized menus for all residents; however, alternatives aligned with individual needs and preferences should be available if the primary menu or immediate selections for a particular meal are not to a resident's liking. Facilities must make reasonable and good faith efforts to develop a menu based on resident requests and resident groups' feedback.

# # #

F804—Nutritive Value/Appear Palatable/Prefer Temp

FOR VOICES FOR QUALITY CARE ADVOCATES

Advocates should be alert to the placement of water cups and other food and drink items. We often see water cups placed on bedside tables. Those tables are then moved out of the way for care issues and not replaced in a position allowing the resident to reach the water cup.

THE REGULATIONS

§483.60(d) Food *and drink*

Each resident receives and the facility provides—

§483.60(d)(1) Food prepared by methods that conserve nutritive value, flavor, and appearance;

§483.60(d)(2) Food *and drink* that is palatable, attractive, and *at a safe and appetizing* temperature.

DEFINITIONS

"Food attractiveness"

refers to the appearance of the food when served to residents.

"Food palatability"

refers to the taste and/or flavor of the food.

"Proper (safe and appetizing) temperature"

means both appetizing to the resident and minimizing the risk for scalding and burns.

INTENT

To assure that the nutritive value of food is not compromised and destroyed because of prolonged:

- (1) Food storage, light, and air exposure; or
- (2) Cooking of foods in a large volume of water; or
- (3) Holding on steam table.

GUIDANCE: EXERPTS FROM THE SURVEYOR'S GUIDELINES

Food should be palatable, attractive, and at **an appetizing** temperature as determined by the type of food to ensure resident's satisfaction, **while minimizing the risk for scalding and burns.**

Providing palatable, attractive, and appetizing food and drink to residents can help to encourage residents to increase the amount they eat and drink. Improved nutrition and hydration status can help prevent, or aid in the recovery from, illness or injury.

###

F805—Food in Form to Meet Individual Needs

THE REGULATIONS

Each resident receives and the facility provides—

§483.*60*(d)(3) Food prepared in a form designed to meet individual needs.

###

F806—Resident Allergies, Preferences and Substitutes

THE REGULATIONS

§483.*60*(d) Food *and drink*

Each resident receives and the facility provides—

§483.*60(d)(4) Food that accommodates resident allergies, intolerances, and preferences;*

§483.*60(d)(5) Appealing options* of similar nutritive value to residents who *choose not to eat* food *that is initially* served or *who request a different meal choice; and*

GUIDANCE: EXERPTS FROM THE SURVEYOR'S GUIDELINES

Facilities should be aware of each resident's allergies, intolerances, and preferences, and provide an appropriate alternative. A food substitute should be consistent with the usual and/or ordinary food items provided by the facility. For example, the facility may, instead of grapefruit juice, substitute another citrus juice or vitamin C rich juice the resident likes.

#

F807—Drinks Avail to Meet Needs/Preferences/Hydration

FOR VOICES FOR QUALITY CARE ADVOCATES

Advocates should be alert to the placement of water cups and other food and drink items. We often see water cups placed on bedside tables. Those tables are then moved out of the way for care issues and not replaced in a position allowing the resident to reach the water cup.

THE REGULATIONS

§483.*60*(d) Food *and drink*

Each resident receives and the facility provides—

§483.*60(d)(6) Drinks, including water and other liquids consistent with resident needs and preferences and sufficient to maintain resident hydration.*

GUIDANCE: EXERPTS FROM THE SURVEYOR'S GUIDELINES

Proper hydration alone is a critical aspect of nutrition among nursing home residents. Individuals who do not receive adequate fluids are more susceptible to urinary tract infection. *pneumonia, decubitus ulcers, skin infections, confusion and disorientation.*

Other food items may also include items that become a liquid at room temperature, such as popsicles and ice cream.

###

F808—Therapeutic Diet Prescribed by Physician

THE REGULATIONS

§483.*60*(e) Therapeutic Diets

§483.*60*(e)(1) Therapeutic diets must be prescribed by the attending physician.

§483.60(e)*(2) The attending physician may delegate to a registered or licensed dietitian the task of prescribing a resident's diet, including a therapeutic diet, to the extent allowed by State law.*

###

F809—Frequency of Meals/Snacks at Bedtime

THE REGULATIONS

§483.*60*(f) Frequency of Meals

§483.*60*(f)(1) Each resident must receive and the facility must provide at least three meals daily, at regular times comparable to normal mealtimes in the community *or in accordance with resident needs, preferences, requests, and plan of care.*

§483.*60*(f)(2)There must be no more than 14 hours between a substantial evening meal and breakfast the following day, except when a nourishing snack is *served* at bedtime, up to 16 hours may elapse between a substantial evening meal and breakfast the following day if a resident group agrees to this meal span.

§483.*60*(f)*(3) Suitable, nourishing alternative meals and snacks must be provided to residents who want to eat at non-traditional times or outside of scheduled meal service times, consistent with the resident plan of care.*

DEFINITIONS

A "Nourishing snack"

means items from the basic food groups, *either singly or in combination with each other.*

"Suitable and nourishing alternative meals and snacks"

means that when an alternate meal or snack is provided, it is of similar nutritive value as the meal or snack offered at the normally scheduled time and consistent with the resident plan of care.

GUIDANCE: EXERPTS FROM THE SURVEYOR'S GUIDELINES

Facility staff must ensure meals and snacks are served at times in accordance with resident's needs, preferences, and requests. Suitable and nourishing alternative meals and snacks must be provided for residents who want to eat at non-traditional times or outside of scheduled meal times. Adequacy of the "nourishing snack" will be determined both by resident interviews and by evaluation of the overall nutritional status of residents in the facility, (for example: Is the offered snack usually satisfying?)

This regulation is not intended to require facilities to provide a 24-hour-a-day full service food operation or an on-site chef. Suitable alternatives may be meals prepared in advance that can be appropriately served by appropriately trained facility staff at non-traditional times.

###

F810—Assistive Devices-Eating Equipment/Utensils

THE REGULATIONS

§483.*60*(g) Assistive devices

The facility must provide special eating equipment and utensils for residents who need them *and appropriate assistance to ensure that the resident can use the assistive devices when consuming meals and snacks.*

GUIDANCE: EXERPTS FROM THE SURVEYOR'S GUIDELINES

The facility must provide appropriate assistive devices to residents who need them to maintain or improve their ability to eat or drink independently, for example, improving poor grasp by enlarging silverware handles with foam padding, aiding residents with impaired coordination or tremor by installing plate guards, or specialized cups. The facility must also provide the *appropriate staff assistance to ensure that these residents can use the assistive devices when eating or drinking.*

For concerns regarding the use of other types of assistive devices, such as postural supports for head, trunk and arms, please see guidance under F676 and F677 for ADL care and services.

###

F811—Feeding Asst—
Training/Supervision/Resident

THE REGULATIONS

§483.*60*(h) Paid feeding assistants-

§483.*60*(h)(1) State approved training course. A facility may use a paid feeding assistant, as defined in § 488.301 of this chapter, if—

- (i) The feeding assistant has successfully completed a State-approved training course that meets the requirements of §483.160 before feeding residents; and
- (ii) The use of feeding assistants is consistent with State law.

§483.*60*(h)(2) Supervision.

- (i) A feeding assistant must work under the supervision of a registered nurse (RN) or licensed practical nurse (LPN).
- (ii) In an emergency, a feeding assistant must call a supervisory nurse for help.

§483.*60*(h)(3) Resident selection criteria.

- (i) A facility must ensure that a feeding assistant **provides dining assistance only** for residents who have no complicated feeding problems.
- (ii) Complicated feeding problems include, but are not limited to, difficulty swallowing, recurrent lung aspirations, and tube or parenteral/IV feedings.
- (iii) The facility must base resident selection on the **interdisciplinary team's** assessment and the resident's latest assessment and plan of care. **Appropriateness for this program should be reflected in the comprehensive care plan.**

NOTE: Paid feeding assistants must complete a training program with the following minimum content as specified at §483.160.

- a. Minimum training course contents. A State-approved training course for paid feeding assistants must include, at a minimum, 8 hours of training in the following:
  - (1) Feeding techniques;
  - (2) Assistance with feeding and hydration;
  - (3) Communication and interpersonal skills;
  - (4) Appropriate responses to resident behavior;
  - (5) Safety and emergency procedures, including the Heimlich maneuver;
  - (6) Infection control;
  - (7) Resident rights; and
  - (8) Recognizing changes in residents that are inconsistent with their normal behavior and the importance of reporting those changes to the supervisory nurse.
- b. Maintenance of records. A facility must maintain a record of all individuals, used by the facility as feeding assistants, who have successfully completed the training course for paid feeding assistants.

DEFINITIONS

"Paid feeding assistant"

is defined in the regulation at 42 CFR §488.301 as "an individual who meets the requirements specified at 42 CFR §483.60(h)(1)(i) and who is paid **by the facility** to feed residents, or who is used under an arrangement with another agency or organization."

NOTE: The regulation uses the term "paid feeding assistant." While we are not using any other term, facilities and States may use whatever term they prefer, such as dining assistant, meal assistant, resident assistant, nutritional aide, etc. in order to convey more respect for the resident. Facilities may identify this position with other titles; however, the facility must be able to identify those employees who meet the requirements under the paid feeding assistant regulation. *While the facility is still responsible for ensuring the safety and care of all residents, this regulation does not apply to family members or to volunteers*

INTENT

To ensure that residents are assessed for appropriateness for a feeding assistant program, receive services as per their plan of care, and feeding assistants are trained and supervised. The use of paid feeding assistants is intended to supplement certified nurse aides, not substitute for nurse aides or licensed nursing staff.

###

F812—Food Procurement Store/Prepare/Serv— Sanitary

FOR VOICES FOR QUALITY CARE ADVOCATES

Advocates working in a situation where this set of regulations is relevant should check the Surveyor's Guidelines. There is a considerable amount of information on the safe handling of food with charts indicating avoidance of potential Foodborne Illnesses.

THE REGULATIONS

§483.60(i) *Food safety requirements.*

The facility must –

§483.**60**(i)(1) - Procure food from sources approved or considered satisfactory by federal, state or local authorities.

- *(i) This may include food items obtained directly from local producers, subject to applicable State and local laws or regulations.*
- *(ii) This provision does not prohibit or prevent facilities from using produce grown in facility gardens, subject to compliance with applicable safe growing and food-handling practices.*
- *(iii) This provision does not preclude residents from consuming foods not procured by the facility.*

§483.**60**(i)(2) - Store, prepare, distribute and serve food *in accordance with professional standards for food service safety.*

###

F813—Personal Food Policy

THE REGULATIONS

§483.60(i) *Food Safety Requirements*

The facility must –

§483.60(i)(3) Have a policy regarding use and storage of foods brought to residents by family and other visitors to ensure safe and sanitary storage, handling, and consumption.

GUIDANCE: EXERPTS FROM THE SURVEYOR'S GUIDELINES

The facility must have a policy regarding food brought to residents by family and other visitors. The policy must also include ensuring facility staff assists the resident in accessing and consuming the food, if the resident is not able to do so on his or her own. The facility also is responsible for storing food brought in by family or visitors in a way that is either separate or easily distinguishable from facility food.

The facility has a responsibility to help family and visitors understand safe food handling practices (such as safe cooling/reheating processes, hot/cold holding temperatures, preventing cross contamination, hand hygiene, etc.). If the facility is assisting family or visitors with reheating or other preparation activities, facility staff must use safe food handling practices

#

F814—Dispose Garbage & Refuse Properly

THE REGULATIONS

§483.**60**(i) *Food Safety Requirements*

The facility must –

§483.**60(i)(4)**- Dispose of garbage and refuse properly.

###

483.65 Specialized Rehabilitative Services

See the Surveyor's Guidelines for information on this F-Tag.

https://www.cms.gov/Medicare/Provider-Enrollment-and-Certification/GuidanceforLawsAndRegulations/Downloads/Advance-Appendix-PP-Including-Phase-2-.pdf

F825—Provide/Obtain Specialized Rehab Services

F826—Rehab Services—Physician Order/Qualified Person

483.70 Administration

See the Surveyor's Guidelines for information on this F-Tag.

https://www.cms.gov/Medicare/Provider-Enrollment-and-Certification/GuidanceforLawsAndRegulations/Downloads/Advance-Appendix-PP-Including-Phase-2-.pdf

F835—Administration

F836—License/Comply w/Fed/State/Local Law/Prof Std

F837—Governing Body

F838—Facility Assessment

F839—Staff Qualifications

F840—Use of Outside Resources

F841—Responsibilities of Medical Director

F842—Resident Records—Identifiable Information

F843—Transfer Agreement

F844—Disclosure of Ownership Requirements

F845—Facility closure—Administrator

F846—Responsibilities of Medical Director

F849—Hospice Services

F850—Qualifications of Social Worker>120 Beds

F851—Payroll Based Journal

483.75 Quality Assurance and Performance Improvement

See the Surveyor's Guidelines for information on this F-Tag.

https://www.cms.gov/Medicare/Provider-Enrollment-and-Certification/GuidanceforLawsAndRegulations/Downloads/Advance-Appendix-PP-Including-Phase-2-.pdf

F865—QAPI Program/Plan, Disclosure/Good Faith Attempt

F866—{PHASE—3} QAPI/QAA Data Collection and Monitoring

F867—QAPI/QAA Improvement Activities

F868—QAA Committee

483.80 Infection Control

F880—Infection Prevention & Control

THE REGULATIONS

§483.*80* Infection Control

The facility must establish and maintain an infection **prevention and** control program designed to provide a safe, sanitary and comfortable environment and to help prevent the development and transmission of **communicable** diseases and infections.

§483.*80(a)* Infection **prevention and** control program.

The facility must establish an infection **prevention and** control program **(IPCP) that must include, at a minimum, the following elements:**

§483.*80(a)(1) A system for preventing, identifying, reporting, investigating, and controlling infections and communicable diseases for all residents, staff, volunteers, visitors, and other individuals providing services under a contractual arrangement based upon the facility assessment conducted according to §483.70(e) and following accepted national standards*;

§483.*80(a)(2) Written standards, policies, and procedures for the program, which must include, but are not limited to:*

- *(i) A system of surveillance designed to identify possible communicable diseases or infections before they can spread to other persons in the facility;*
- *(ii) When and to whom possible incidents of communicable disease or infections should be reported;*
- *(iii) Standard and transmission-based precautions to be followed to prevent spread of infections;*

- *(iv) When and how isolation should be used for a resident; including but not limited to:*
  - ○ *(A) The type and duration of the isolation, depending upon the infectious agent or organism involved, and*
  - ○ *(B) A requirement that the isolation should be the least restrictive possible for the resident under the circumstances.*

(v) The circumstances under which the facility must prohibit employees with a communicable disease or infected skin lesions from direct contact with residents or their food, if direct contact will transmit the disease; *and*

(vi) The hand hygiene procedures to be followed by staff involved in direct resident contact.

§483.*80(a)(4) A system for recording incidents identified under the facility's IPCP and the corrective actions taken by the facility.*

§483.*80(e)* Linens.

Personnel must handle, store, process, and transport linens so as to prevent the spread of infection.

§483.*80(f) Annual review.*

The facility will conduct an annual review of its IPCP and update their program, as necessary.

DEFINITIONS

"Airborne precautions":

actions taken to prevent or minimize the transmission of infectious agents/organisms that remain infectious over long distances when suspended in the air. These infectious particles can remain suspended in the air for prolonged periods of time and can be carried on normal air currents in a room or beyond, to adjacent spaces or areas receiving exhaust air.40

"Alcohol-based handrub (ABHR)":

a 60-95 percent ethanol or isopropyl alcohol- containing preparation base designed for application to the hands to reduce the number of viable microorganisms.

"Cleaning":

removal of visible soil (e.g., organic and inorganic material) from objects and surfaces and is normally accomplished manually or mechanically using water with detergents or enzymatic products.

"Cohorting":

the practice of grouping residents infected or colonized with the same infectious agent together to confine their care to one area and prevent contact with susceptible residents (cohorting residents).40   During outbreaks, healthcare **staff** may be assigned to a **specific** cohort of residents to further limit opportunities for transmission (cohorting staff). *The terms "cohort or cohorting" is standardized language used in the practice of infection prevention and control; the use of this terminology is not intended to offend residents or staff.*

"Colonization":

the presence of microorganisms on or within body sites without detectable host immune response, cellular damage, or clinical expression. 40

"Communicable disease"

(also known as [a.k.a.] "contagious disease"): an infection transmissible (*e.g.,* from person-to-person) by direct contact with an affected individual or the individual's body fluids or by indirect means (e.g., contaminated object).

"Community-*acquired* infections"

(a.k.a. "present on admission"): infections that are present or incubating at the time of admission and *which* generally develop within 72 hours of admission.

"Contact precautions":

measures that are intended to prevent transmission of infectious agents which are spread by direct or indirect contact with the resident or the resident's environment.

"Contaminated laundry":

laundry which has been soiled with blood/body fluids or other potentially infectious materials or may contain sharps.

"Decontamination":

the use of physical or chemical means to remove, inactivate, or destroy pathogenic organisms on a surface or item to the point where they are no longer capable of transmitting infectious particles and the surface or item is rendered safe for handling, use, or disposal.

"Disinfectant":

usually a chemical agent (but sometimes a physical agent) that destroys disease- causing pathogens or other harmful microorganisms but might not kill bacterial spores. It refers to substances applied to inanimate objects.

"Disinfection":

thermal or chemical destruction of pathogenic and other types of microorganisms. Disinfection is less lethal than sterilization because it destroys most recognized pathogenic microorganisms but not necessarily all microbial forms (e.g., bacterial spores).

"Droplet precautions":

actions designed to reduce/prevent the transmission of pathogens spread through close respiratory or mucous membrane contact with respiratory secretions.

"Hand hygiene":

a general term that applies to *hand washing*, antiseptic *hand wash, and alcohol-based hand rub.*

"Hand washing":

the vigorous, brief rubbing together of all surfaces of hands with plain (i.e., nonantimicrobial) soap and water, followed by rinsing under a stream of water.

"Healthcare-associated infection (HAI)":

an infection that *residents acquire, that is associated with a medical or surgical intervention (e.g., podiatry, wound care debridement) within a nursing home and was not present or incubating at the time of admission.*

"Hygienically clean":

being free of pathogens in sufficient numbers to cause human illness.

"Infection":

the establishment of an infective agent in or on a suitable host, producing clinical signs and symptoms (e.g., fever, redness, heat, purulent exudates, etc.).

"Infection preventionist":

term used for the person(s) designated by the facility to be responsible for the infection prevention and control program. NOTE: Designation of a specific individual, detailed training, qualifications, and hourly requirements for an infection preventionist are not required until implementation of Phase 3.

"Personal protective equipment (PPE)": protective items or garments worn to protect the body or clothing from hazards that can cause injury *and to protect residents from cross-transmission.*

"(Regulated) Medical waste":

liquid or semi-liquid blood or other potentially infectious materials; contaminated items that would release blood or other potentially infectious materials in a liquid or semi-liquid state if compressed; items that are caked with dried blood or other potentially infectious materials and are capable of releasing these materials during handling (e.g., blood-soaked bandages); contaminated sharps.

NOTE: Authorities having jurisdiction may have more stringent regulations than OSHA.

"Standard Precautions":

infection prevention practices that apply to all residents, regardless of suspected or confirmed diagnosis or presumed infection status. *Standard precautions is based on the principle that all blood, body fluids, secretions, excretions except sweat, regardless of whether they contain visible blood, non-intact skin, and mucous membranes may contain transmissible infectious agents. Furthermore, equipment or items in the patient environment likely to have been contaminated with infectious body fluids must be handled in a manner to prevent transmission of infectious agents. Standard precautions include but are not limited to hand hygiene; use of gloves, gown, mask, eye protection, or face shield, depending on the anticipated exposure; safe injection practices, and respiratory hygiene/cough etiquette. Also, equipment or items in the patient environment likely to have been contaminated with infectious body fluids must be handled in a manner to prevent transmission of infectious agents (e.g., wear gloves for direct contact, properly clean and disinfect or sterilize reusable equipment before use on another patient).*

"Transmission-based precautions"

(a.k.a. "Isolation Precautions"): actions (precautions) implemented, in addition to standard precautions, that are based upon the means of transmission (airborne, contact, and droplet) in order to prevent or control infections. **NOTE: Although the regulatory language refers to "isolation," the nomenclature widely accepted and used in this guidance will refer to "transmission-based precautions" instead of "isolation".**

•

INTENT

The intent of this regulation is to ensure that the facility:

- Develops and implementsan ongoing infection prevention and control program (IPCP) to prevent, recognize, and control the onset and spread of infection to the extent possible and reviews and updates the IPCP annually and as necessary. This would include revision of the IPCP as national standards change;

- Establishes facility-wide systems for the prevention, identification, investigation and control of infections of residents, staff, and visitors. It must include an ongoing system of surveillance designed to identify possible communicable diseases or infections before they can spread to other persons in the facility and procedures for reporting possible incidents of communicable disease or infections; NOTE: For purposes of this guidance, "staff" includes *employees, consultants, contractors, volunteers, caregivers who provide care and services to residents on behalf of the facility, and students in the facility's nurse aide training programs or from affiliated academic institutions.*

- *Develops and implements written policies and procedures for infection control that, at a minimum:*
  - *Explain how standard precautions and when transmission-based precautions should be utilized, including but not limited to the type and duration of precautions for particular infections or organisms involved and that the precautions should be the least restrictive possible for the resident given the circumstances and the resident's ability to follow the precautions;*

    ○ *Prohibit staff with a communicable disease or infected skin lesions from direct contact with residents or their food, if direct contact will transmit the disease; and*

    ○ *Require staff follow hand hygiene practices consistent with accepted standards of practice.*

- *Requires staff handle, store, process, and transport all linens and laundry in accordance with accepted national standards in order to produce hygienically clean laundry and prevent the spread of infection to the extent possible.*

###

F881—Antibiotics Stewardship Program

THE REGULATIONS

§483.80(a) *Infection prevention and control program.*

The facility must establish an infection prevention and control program (IPCP) that must include, at a minimum, the following elements:

§483.80(a)(3) *An antibiotic stewardship program that includes antibiotic use protocols and a system to monitor antibiotic use.*

DEFINITIONS

"Antibiotic":

a medication used to treat bacterial infections. They are not effective for infections caused by viruses (e.g., influenza or most cases of bronchitis).

"Antibiotic Stewardship":

refers to a set of commitments and actions designed to optimize the treatment of infections while reducing the adverse events associated with antibiotic use.62 This can be accomplished through improving antibiotic prescribing, administration, and management practices thus reducing inappropriate use to ensure that residents receive the right antibiotic for the right indication, dose, and duration.

"Clostridium difficile infection (C. difficile or CDI)":

an infection from a bacterium that causes colitis, an inflammation of the colon, causing diarrhea.

"Colonization":

the presence of microorganisms on or within body sites without detectable host immune response, cellular damage, or clinical expression.

"Methicillin-resistant Staphylococcus aureus (MRSA)" (a.k.a. Oxacillin-resistant Staphylococcus aureus):

Staphylococcus aureus bacteria that are resistant to treatment with one of the semi-synthetic penicillins (e.g., Oxacillin/Nafcillin/Methicillin).

"Multidrug-Resistant Organisms (MDROs)":

microorganisms, predominantly bacteria, that are resistant to one or more classes of antimicrobial agents.51 Although the names of certain MDROs describe resistance to only one agent, these pathogens are frequently resistant to most available antimicrobial agents and include multidrug-resistant gram negative bacteria (GNB), Carbapenem-resistant Enterobacteriaceae (CRE), and extended spectrum beta-lactamase- producing Enterobacteriaceae (ESBLs).

"Vancomycin resistant enterococcus (VRE)":

species of enterococcus which have developed resistance to the antibiotic, vancomycin.

GUIDANCE: EXERPTS FROM THE SURVEYOR'S GUIDELINES

Nursing home residents are at risk for adverse outcomes associated with the inappropriate use of antibiotics that may include but are not limited to the following:

- Increased adverse drug events and drug interactions (e.g., allergic rash, anaphylaxis or death);
- Serious diarrheal infections from C. difficile;
- Disruption of normal flora (e.g., this can result in overgrowth of Candida such as oral thrush); and/or
- Colonization and/or infection with antibiotic-resistant organisms such as MRSA, VRE, and multidrug-resistant GNB.

294

F882—{PHASE—3} Infection Preventionist Qualifications/Role

FOR VOICES FOR QUALITY CARE ADVOCATES

NOTE: This regulation does not go into effect until Phase 3 is implemented.

THE REGULATIONS

§483.80(b) Infection preventionist

[§483.80(b) and all subparts will be implemented beginning November 28, 2019 (Phase 3)] The facility must designate one or more individual(s) as the infection preventionist(s) (IP)(s) who are responsible for the facility's IPCP. The IP must:

§483.80(b)(1) Have primary professional training in nursing, medical technology, microbiology, epidemiology, or other related field;

§483.80(b)(2) Be qualified by education, training, experience or certification;

§483.80(b)(3) Work at least part-time at the facility; and

§483.80(b)(4) Have completed specialized training in infection prevention and control.

§483.80 (c) IP participation on quality assessment and assurance committee. The individual designated as the IP, or at least one of the individuals if there is more than one IP, must be a member of the facility's quality assessment and assurance committee and report to the committee on the IPCP on a regular basis.

#

F883—Influenza and Pneumococcal Immunizations

THE REGULATIONS

§483.80(d) Influenza and pneumococcal immunizations

§483.80(d)(1) Influenza. The facility must develop policies and procedures to ensure that-

- (i) Before offering the influenza immunization, each resident or the resident's representative receives education regarding the benefits and potential side effects of the immunization;
- (ii) Each resident is offered an influenza immunization October 1 through March 31 annually, unless the immunization is medically contraindicated or the resident has already been immunized during this time period;
- (iii) The resident or the resident's representative has the opportunity to refuse immunization; and
- (iv) The resident's medical record includes documentation that indicates, at a minimum, the following:
    - (A) That the resident or resident's representative was provided education regarding the benefits and potential side effects of influenza immunization; and
    - (B) That the resident either received the influenza immunization or did not receive the influenza immunization due to medical contraindications or refusal.

§483.*80(d)(2)* Pneumococcal disease. The facility must develop policies and procedures to ensure that-

- (i) Before offering the pneumococcal immunization, each resident or the resident's representative receives education regarding the benefits and potential side effects of the immunization;
- (ii) Each resident is offered a pneumococcal immunization, unless the immunization is medically contraindicated or the resident has already been immunized;

- (iii) The resident or the resident's representative has the opportunity to refuse immunization; and
- (iv) The resident's medical record includes documentation that indicates, at a minimum, the following:
  - o (A) That the resident or resident's representative was provided education regarding the benefits and potential side effects of pneumococcal immunization; and
  - o (B) That the resident either received the pneumococcal immunization or did not receive the pneumococcal immunization due to medical contraindication or refusal.

INTENT

The intent of this regulation is to:

- Minimize the risk of residents acquiring, transmitting, or experiencing complications from influenza and pneumococcal disease by *ensuring* that each resident:
  - o Is informed about the benefits and risks of immunizations; and
  - o Has the opportunity to receive the influenza and pneumococcal vaccine(s), unless medically contraindicated, refused or was already immunized.
- *Ensure* documentation in the resident's medical record of the information/education provided regarding the benefits and risks of immunization and the administration or the refusal of or medical contraindications to the vaccine(s).

###

###

F907—Space and Equipment

THE REGULATIONS

§483.**90**(d) Space and Equipment

The facility must--

§483.**90**(d)(1) Provide sufficient space and equipment in dining, health services, recreation, and program areas to enable staff to provide residents with needed services as required by these standards and as identified in each resident's *assessment and* plan of care; and

INTENT

The intent of this regulation is to ensure that dining, health services, recreation, activities and programs areas are large enough to comfortably accommodate the needs of the residents who usually occupy this space.

Dining, health services, recreation, and program areas should be large enough to comfortably accommodate the persons who usually occupy that space, including the wheelchairs, walkers, and other ambulating aids used by the many residents who require more than standard movement spaces. **"Sufficient space"** means the resident can access the area, it is not functionally off- limits, and the resident's functioning is not restricted once access to the space is gained.

Program areas where resident groups engage in activities focused on manipulative skills and hand-eye coordination should have sufficient space for storage of their supplies and "works in progress."

Program areas where residents receive physical therapy should have sufficient space and equipment to meet the needs of the resident's therapy requirement.

"Recreation/activities area" means any area where residents can participate in those activities identified in their plan of care.

#

F908—Essential Equipment, Safe Operating Condition

THE REGULATIONS

§483.**90**(d)(2) Maintain all mechanical, electrical, and patient care equipment in safe operating condition.

#

F909—Resident Bed

THE REGULATIONS

§483.**90**(d)(3) *Conduct Regular inspection of all bed frames, mattresses, and bed rails, if any, as part of a regular maintenance program to identify areas of possible entrapment. When bed rails and mattresses are used and purchased separately from the bed frame, the facility must ensure that the bed rails, mattress, and bed frame are compatible.*

#

F910—Resident Room

THE REGULATIONS

§483.**90**(e) Resident Rooms

Resident rooms must be designed and equipped for adequate nursing care, comfort, and privacy of residents.

###

F911—Bedroom Number of Residents

THE REGULATIONS

§483.**90** (e)(1) Bedrooms must

§483.**90**(e)(1)(i) Accommodate no more than four residents. ***For facilities that receive approval of construction or reconstruction plans by State and local authorities or are newly certified after November 28, 2016, bedrooms must accommodate no more than two residents.***

###

F912—Bedrooms Measure at Least 80 Square Ft/Resident

THE REGULATIONS

§483.90(e)(1)(ii) Measure at least 80 square feet per resident in multiple resident bedrooms, and at least 100 square feet in single resident rooms;

GUIDANCE: EXERPTS FROM THE SURVEYOR'S GUIDELINES

The measurement of the square footage should be based upon the useable living space of the room. Therefore, the minimum square footage in resident rooms should be measured based upon the floor's measurements exclusive of toilets and bath areas, closets, lockers, wardrobes, alcoves, or vestibules. However, if the height of the alcoves or vestibules reasonably provides useful living area, then the corresponding floor area may be included in the calculation.

The space occupied by movable wardrobes should be excluded from the useable square footage in a room unless it is an item of the resident's own choice and it is in addition to the individual closet space in the resident's room. Non-permanent items of the resident's own choice should have no effect in the calculation of useable living space.

###

F913—Bedrooms Have Direct Access to Exit Corridor

THE REGULATIONS

§483.**90**(e)(1)(iii) Have direct access to an exit corridor;

GUIDANCE: EXERPTS FROM THE SURVEYOR'S GUIDELINES

Each resident bedroom shall be individually accessible from the corridor without passing through another room.

###

F914—Bedrooms Assure Full Visual Privacy

THE REGULATIONS

§483.90(e)(1)(iv) Be designed or equipped to assure full visual privacy for each resident;

§483.90(e)(1)(v) In facilities initially certified after March 31, 1992, except in private rooms, each bed must have ceiling suspended curtains, which extend around the bed to provide total visual privacy in combination with adjacent walls and curtains.

GUIDANCE: EXERPTS FROM THE SURVEYOR'S GUIDELINES

"Full visual privacy" means that residents have a means of completely withdrawing from public view, without staff assistance, while occupying their bed (e.g., curtain, moveable screens, private room).

The guidelines do not intend to limit the provisions of privacy to solely one or more curtains, movable screens or a private room. Facility operators are free to use other means to provide full visual privacy, with those means varying according to the needs and requests of residents. However, the requirement explicitly states that bedrooms must "be designed or equipped to assure full visual privacy for each resident." For example, a resident with a bed by the window cannot be required to remain out of his or her room while his/her roommate is having a dressing change. Room design or equipment must provide privacy.

###

F915—Resident Room Window

THE REGULATIONS

§483.**90(a)(7)** *Buildings must have an outside window or outside door in every sleeping room, and for any building constructed after July 5, 2016 the sill height must not exceed 36 inches above the floor. Windows in atrium walls are considered outside windows for the purposes of this requirement.*

§483.**90**(e)(1)(vi) - Resident Rooms Bedrooms must --

§483.**90**(e)(1)(vi) - Have at least one window to the outside; and

GUIDANCE: EXERPTS FROM THE SURVEYOR'S GUIDELINES

Every resident/patient sleeping room shall have an outside window. A facility with resident room windows, as defined by K381, or that open to an outside atrium such as a courtyard in accordance with Life Safety Code, can meet this requirement for a window to the outside. Windows facing an interior atrium, skylights, etc., do not meet this requirement.

In addition to conforming to the Life Safety Code, this requirement was included to assist the resident's orientation to day and night, weather, and general awareness of space outside the facility. The facility is required to provide for a "safe, clean, comfortable and homelike environment" by deemphasizing the institutional character of the setting, to the extent possible. Windows are an important aspect in assuring the homelike environment of a facility.

#

F916—Resident Room Floor Above Grade

THE REGULATIONS

§483.**90**(e)(1)(vii) Have a floor at or above grade level.

GUIDANCE: EXERPTS FROM THE SURVEYOR'S GUIDELINES

"At or above grade level" means a room in which the room floor is at or above the surrounding exterior ground level. No resident rooms in basements or below ground level are allowed.

###

F917—Resident Room Bed/Furniture/Closet

THE REGULATIONS

§483.*10(i)(4)* Private closet space in each resident room, as specified in §483.*90* (e)(2)(iv)

§483.*90*(e)(2) -The facility must provide each resident with--

- (i) A separate bed of proper size and height for the *safety and* convenience of the resident;
- (ii) A clean, comfortable mattress;
- (iii) Bedding, appropriate to the weather and climate; and
- (iv) Functional furniture appropriate to the resident's needs, and individual closet space in the resident's bedroom with clothes racks and shelves accessible to the resident.

§483.*90*(e)(3) CMS, or in the case of a nursing facility the survey agency, may permit variations in requirements specified in paragraphs (e)(1) (i) and (ii) of this section relating to rooms in individual cases when the facility demonstrates in writing that the variations

- (i) Are in accordance with the special needs of the residents; and
- (ii) Will not adversely affect residents' health and safety.

GUIDANCE: EXERPTS FROM THE SURVEYOR'S GUIDELINES

"Functional furniture appropriate to the resident's needs" means that the furniture in each resident's room contributes to the resident attaining or maintaining his or her highest practicable level of independence and well-being. In general, furnishings include a place to put clothing away in an organized manner that will let it remain clean, free of wrinkles, and accessible to the resident while protecting it from casual access by others;

a place to put personal effects such as pictures and a bedside clock, and furniture suitable for the comfort of the resident and visitors (e.g., a chair).

"Clothes racks and shelves accessible to the resident" means that residents can get to and reach their hanging clothing whenever they choose.

"Private closet space" means that each resident's clothing is kept separate from clothing of roommate(s).

The term "closet space" is not necessarily limited to a space installed into the wall. For some facilities without such installed closets, compliance may be attained through the use of storage furniture such as wardrobes. Out-of-season items may be stored in alternate locations outside the resident's room.

A variation must be in accordance with the special needs of the residents and must not adversely affect the health or safety of residents. Facility hardship is not part of the basis for granting a variation. Since the special needs of residents may change periodically, or different residents may be transferred into a room that has been granted a variation, variations must be reviewed and considered for renewal whenever the facility is certified. If the needs of the residents within the room have not changed since the last annual inspection, the variance should continue if the facility so desires.

F918—Bedrooms Equipped/Near Lavatory/Toilet

THE REGULATIONS

§483.*90*(f) *Bathroom* Facilities

Each resident room must be equipped with or located near toilet and bathing facilities. *For facilities that receive approval of construction or reconstruction plans from State and local authorities or are newly certified after November 28, 2016, each residential room must have its own bathroom equipped with at least a commode and sink.*

GUIDANCE: EXERPTS FROM THE SURVEYOR'S GUIDELINES

"Bathing Facilities" is defined as a space that contains either a shower(s) or a tub(s) for resident use. See definition of "toilet facilities" for definition of "located near."

"Reconstruction" means that the facility undergoes reconfiguration of the space such that the space is not permitted to be occupied, or the entire building or and an entire occupancy with the building, such as a wing of the building is modified. The requirement applies to the reconstructed area, so that where reconstruction involves a limited area within a building, we would not expect the entire building to upgrade to the new requirements *of each resident room being equipped or located near toilet and bathing facilities.*

"Toilet facilities" is defined as a space that contains a lavatory and a toilet/*commode. CMS is also using the term "commode" to mean the same as a "toilet" when referring to a plumbing fixture*. If the resident's room is not equipped with an adjoining toilet facility, then "located near" means residents who are independent in the use of a toilet/**commode**, including chair bound residents, can routinely use a toilet/commode in the unit *that they can access quickly*.

When a facility undergoes a change of ownership under §489.18 and the new owner does not accept assignment of the existing provider agreement and requires a "new initial certification" for a new provider agreement that would be effective after November 28, 2016, the facility would be expected to be upgraded to meet these new requirements of each resident bedroom to have its own bathroom consisting of at least a sink and commode/toilet. This would also apply when the provider agreement was terminated by CMS and another provider is working to reopen the facility.

Each resident room must be equipped with or located near toilet/commode and bathing facilities. For facilities that receive approval of construction or reconstruction plans from State and local authorities or are newly certified after November 28, 2016, each resident room must have its own bathroom equipped with at least a commode, and sink.

F919—Resident Call System

THE REGULATIONS

§483.90(g) Resident Call System

The facility must be adequately equipped to allow residents to call for staff assistance through a communication system *which relays the call directly to a staff member or to a centralized staff work area.*

§483.90(g)(1) *Each resident's bedside; and*

[483.90(g)(1) will be implemented beginning November 28, 2019 (Phase 3)]

§483.90(g)(2) Toilet and bathing facilities.

GUIDANCE: EXERPTS FROM THE SURVEYOR'S GUIDELINES

This requirement is met only if all portions of the system are functioning (e.g., system is not turned off at the nurses' station, the volume too low to be heard, the light above a room or rooms is not working, no staff at nurses' station), and calls are being answered. For wireless systems, compliance is met only if staff who answer resident calls, have functioning devices in their possession, and are answering resident calls.

#

F920—Requirements for Dining and Activity Rooms

FOR VOICES FOR QUALITY CARE ADVOCATES

See F-584 for the Maryland and Washington D.C. regulations on lighting in nursing homes and assisted living facilities.

THE REGULATIONS

§483.**90**(h) Dining and Resident Activities

The facility must provide one or more rooms designated for resident dining and activities.

These rooms must--

§483.**90**(h)(1) Be well lighted;

§483.**90**(h)(2) Be well ventilated;

§483.**90**(h)(3) Be adequately furnished; and

§483.**90**(h)(4) Have sufficient space to accommodate all activities.

GUIDANCE: EXERPTS FROM THE SURVEYOR'S GUIDELINES

"Well lighted" is defined as levels of illumination that are suitable to tasks performed by a resident.

"Well ventilated" is defined as good air circulation, avoidance of drafts at floor level, and adequate smoke and odor exhaust removal

Reference ASHRAE Standard 179 for ventilation requirements in nursing homes activity and dining areas.

An *"adequately furnished"* dining area accommodates different residents' physical and social needs. An adequately furnished organized activities area accommodates the needs, interests and preferences of its residents.

"Sufficient space to accommodate all activities" means that there is enough space available and it is adaptable to a variety of uses and residents' needs

F921—Safe/Functional/Sanitary/Comfortable Environment

THE REGULATIONS

§483.**90**(i) Other Environmental Conditions

The facility must provide a safe, functional, sanitary, and comfortable environment for residents, staff and the public.

###

F922—Procedures to Ensure Water Availability

THE REGULATIONS

The facility must--

§483.**90**(i)(1) Establish procedures to ensure that water is available to essential areas when there is a loss of normal water supply;

GUIDANCE: EXERPTS FROM THE SURVEYOR'S GUIDELINES

The facility should have a written procedure which defines the source of water when there is a loss of normal water supply, including provisions for storing the water, both potable and nonpotable, a method for distributing the water and a method for estimating the volume of water required.

###

F923—Ventilation

THE REGULATIONS

§483.**90**(i)(2) Have adequate outside ventilation by means of windows, or mechanical ventilation, or a combination of the two.

#

F924—Corridors Have Firmly Secured Handrails

THE REGULATIONS

§483.**90**(i)(3) Equip corridors with firmly secured handrails on each side.

GUIDANCE: EXERPTS FROM THE SURVEYOR'S GUIDELINES

"Secured handrails" means handrails that are firmly affixed to the wall.

#

F925—Maintains Effective Pest Control Program

THE REGULATIONS

§483.**90**(i)(4) Maintain an effective pest control program so that the facility is free of pests and rodents.

GUIDANCE: EXERPTS FROM THE SURVEYOR'S GUIDELINES

An **"effective pest control program"** is defined as measures to eradicate and contain common household pests (e.g., bed bugs, lice, roaches, ants, mosquitoes, flies, mice, and rats).

#

F926—Smoking Policies

FOR VOICES FOR QUALITY CARE ADVOCATES

The regulations under this F-Tag are included in the temporary moratorium on full enforcement.

THE REGULATIONS

§483.**90(i)(5)** *Establish policies, in accordance with applicable Federal, State, and local laws and regulations, regarding smoking, including tobacco cessation, smoking areas and safety, including but limited to non-smoking residents.*

#

483.95 Training Requirements

F940—{PHASE-3} Training Requirements—General

F941—{PHASE-3} Communication Training

F942—{PHASE-3} Resident's Rights Training

F943—Abuse, Neglect, and Exploitation Training

F944—{PHASE-3} QAPI Training

F945—{PHASE-3} Infection Control Training

F946—{PHASE-3} Compliance and Ethics Training

F947—Required In-Service Training for Nurse Aides

F948—Training for Feeding Assistants

F949—{PHASE-3} Behavioral Health Training

Federal Long Term Care Ombudsman Regulations

The Long Term Care Ombudsman Program was established in the Older American's Act of 1965. The regulations for this federal program govern all Long Term Care Ombudsman Offices in every US state and territory including the District of Columbia.

While the primary governing laws and regulations for this program are federal, many states have additional laws and regulations that govern the operations of the program in that state.

This section contains *some* of the current federal regulations that went into effect on July 1, 2016. We have chosen those regulations that are likely to apply to situations our Voices Volunteers are may encounter. Some regulations are quoted directly from the material in the Federal Register. Others are paraphrased for an easier read. The paraphrased items will be presented in *italics*.

The full text of this Rule can be accessed at this URL.

https://www.federalregister.gov/documents/2015/02/11/2015-01914/state-long-term-care-ombudsman-programs

§1327.11 Establishment of the Office of the State Long-Term Care Ombudsman.

(a) The Office of the State Long-Term Care Ombudsman shall be an entity which shall be headed by the State Long-Term Care Ombudsman, who shall carry responsibilities set forth in §1327.13 and shall carry out, directly and/or through local Ombudsman entities, the duties set forth in §1327.19

- **(2)(c)** The State agency shall require that the Ombudsman serve on a full-time basis. In providing leadership and management of the Office, the functions, responsibilities, and duties, as set forth in § 1327.13 and 1327.19 are to constitute the entirety of the

Ombudsman's work. The State agency or other agency carrying out the Office shall not require or request the Ombudsman to be responsible for leading, managing, or performing the work of non-ombudsman services or programs except on a time-limited, intermittent basis.

- o **(1)** This provision does not limit the authority of the Ombudsman program to provide ombudsman services to populations other than residents of long-term care facilities so long as the appropriations under the Act are utilized to serve residents of long-term care facilities, as authorized by the Act.

(d) The State agency, and other entity selecting the Ombudsman, if applicable, shall ensure that the Ombudsman meets minimum qualifications which shall include, but not be limited to demonstrated expertise in:

- o **(1)** Long term services and supports or other direct services for older persons or individuals with disabilities;
- o **(2)** Consumer-oriented public policy advocacy;
- o **(3)** Leadership and program management skills; and
- o **(4)** Negotiation and problem resolution skills.

Policies and Procedures: Independence of the State Ombudsman

The policies and procedures must address the matters within this subsection.

- • **(1)** ... Policies and procedures regarding program administration must include, but not be limited to:
  - o **(i)** A requirement that the agency in which the Office is organizationally located must not have personnel policies or practices which prohibit the Ombudsman from performing the functions and responsibilities of the Ombudsman . . .

Policies and Procedures: State Ombudsman Monitoring of Local Programs

- **(ii)** A requirement that an agency hosting a local Ombudsman entity must not have personnel policies or practices which prohibit a representative of the Office from performing the duties of the Ombudsman program or from adhering to the requirements of section 712 of the Act.. . .
- **(iii)** A requirement that the Ombudsman shall monitor the performance of local Ombudsman entities which the Ombudsman has designated to carry out the duties of the Office.
- **(iv)** A description of the process by which the agencies hosting local Ombudsman entities will coordinate with the Ombudsman in the employment or appointment of representatives of the Office.

Policies and Procedures: Standards For Prompt Response to Complaints

- **(v)** Standards to assure prompt response to complaints by the Office and/or local Ombudsman entities which prioritize abuse, neglect, exploitation, and time sensitive complaints and which consider the severity of the risk to the resident, the imminence of the threat of harm to the resident, and the opportunity for mitigating harm to the resident through provision of Ombudsman Program services.

Policies and Procedures: State Ombudsman Fiscal Oversight

- **(vi)** Procedures that clarify appropriate fiscal responsibilities of the local Ombudsman entity, including but not limited to clarifications regarding access to programmatic fiscal information by appropriate representatives of the Office.

Policies and Procedures: Access to Residents, Facilities, and Records

- **(2)** ... Policies and procedures regarding timely access to facilities, residents, and appropriate records (regardless of format and including, upon request, copies of such records) by the Ombudsman and representatives of the Office must include, but not be limited to:
  - o **(i)** Access to enter all long term care facilities at any time during a facility's regular business hours or regular visiting hours, and at any other time when access may be required by the circumstances to be investigated;
  - o *(ii) Omitted. See the URL for the full Rule at the beginning of this section*
  - o **(iii)** Access to the name and contact information of the resident representative, if any, where needed...
  - o **(iv)**Access to review the medical, social and other records relating to a resident, if—
    - **(A)** The resident or resident representative communicates informed consent to the access and the consent is given in writing or through the use of auxiliary aids and services;
    - **(B)** The resident or resident representative communicates informed consent orally, visually, or through the use of auxiliary aids and services, and such consent is documented contemporaneously by a representative of the Office in accordance with such procedures; and
    - **(C)** Access is necessary in order to investigate a complaint, the resident representative refuses to consent to the access, a representative of the Office has reasonable cause to believe that the resident representative is not acting in the best interests of the resident, and the representative of the Office obtains the approval of the Ombudsman;
  - o **(v)** Access to the administrative records, policies, and documents, to which the residents have, or the general public has access, of long-term care facilities;

o **(vi)** Access of the Ombudsman to, and, upon request, copies of all licensing and certification records maintained by the State with respect to long-term care facilities; and

o **(vii)** Reaffirmation that the Health Insurance Portability and Accountability Act of 1996 (HIPAA)... does not preclude release by covered entities of resident private health information or other resident identifying information to the Ombudsman program, including but not limited to residents' medical, social, or other records, a list of resident names and room numbers, or information collected in the course of a State or Federal survey or inspection process.

Policies and Procedures: Prohibition Against Disclosure of Identifying Information

§ 1327.13(e);

- **(ii)** Prohibition of the disclosure of identifying information of any resident with respect to whom the Ombudsman program maintains files, records, or information,...unless:
  - o **(A)** The resident or the resident representative communicates informed consent to the disclosure and the consent is given in writing or through the use of auxiliary aids and services;
  - o **(B)** The resident or resident representative communicates informed consent orally, visually, or through the use of auxiliary aids and services and such consent is documented contemporaneously by a representative of the Office in accordance with such procedures; or
  - o **(C)** The disclosure is required by court order;
- **(iii)** Prohibition of the disclosure of identifying information of any complainant with respect to whom the Ombudsman program maintains files, records, or information, unless:
  - o **(A)** The complainant communicates informed consent to the disclosure and the consent is given in writing or through the use of auxiliary aids and services;

◦ **(B)** The complainant communicates informed consent orally, visually, or through the use of auxiliary aids and services and such consent is documented contemporaneously by a representative of the Office in accordance with such procedures; or

◦ **(C)** The disclosure is required by court order;

- **(iv)** Exclusion of the Ombudsman and representatives of the Office from abuse reporting requirements, including when such reporting would disclose identifying information of a complainant or resident without appropriate consent or court order, except as otherwise provided. . .

Policies and Procedures: Conflicts of Interest—OMITTED

Policies and Procedures: System Advocacy

(5) Systems Advocacy. Policies and procedures related to systems advocacy must assure that the Office is required and has sufficient authority to carry out its responsibility to analyze, comment on, and monitor the development and implementation of Federal, State, and local laws, regulations, and other government policies and actions that pertain to long-term care facilities and services and to the health, safety, welfare, and rights of residents, and to recommend any changes in such laws, regulations, and policies as the Office determines to be appropriate.

- **(i)** Such procedures must exclude the Ombudsman and representatives of the Office from any State lobbying prohibitions to the extent that such requirements are inconsistent with section 712 of the Act.

- **(ii)** Nothing in this part shall prohibit the Ombudsman or the State agency or other agency in which the Office is organizationally located from establishing policies which promote consultation regarding the determinations of the Office related to recommended changes in laws, regulations, and policies. However, such a policy shall not require a right to review or pre-approve positions or communications of the Office.

Policies and Procedures: Designation of Local Ombudsman Entities

(6) Designation. Policies and procedures related to designation must establish the criteria and process by which the Ombudsman shall designate and refuse, suspend or remove designation of local Ombudsman entities and representatives of the Office.

- **(i)** Such criteria should include, but not be limited to, the authority to refuse, suspend or remove designation a local Ombudsman entity or representative of the Office in situations in which an identified conflict of interest cannot be adequately removed or remedied. . .

Policies and Procedures: Grievance and Disclosure Processes

(7) Grievance process. Policies and procedures related to grievances must establish a grievance process for the receipt and review of grievances regarding the determinations or actions of the Ombudsman and representatives of the Office.

- **(i)** Such process shall include an opportunity for reconsideration of the Ombudsman decision to refuse, suspend, or remove designation of a local Ombudsman entity or representative of the Office. Notwithstanding the grievance process, the Ombudsman shall make the final determination to designate or to refuse, suspend, or remove designation of a local Ombudsman entity or representative of the Office.

(8) Determinations of the Office. Policies and procedures related to the determinations of the Office must ensure that the Ombudsman, as head of the Office, shall be able to independently make determinations and establish positions of the Office, without necessarily representing the determinations or positions of the State agency or other agency in which the Office is organizationally located, regarding:

- **(i)** Disclosure of information maintained by the Ombudsman program within the limitations set forth in section 712(d) of the Act;
- **(ii)** Recommendations to changes in Federal, State and local laws, regulations, policies and actions pertaining to the health, safety, welfare, and rights of residents; and
- **(iii)** Provision of information to public and private agencies, legislators, the media, and other persons, regarding the problems and concerns of residents and recommendations related to the problems and concerns.

Functions and Responsibilities: Investigate and Resolve Complaints

§ 1327.13 Functions and responsibilities of the State Long-Term Care Ombudsman.

The Ombudsman, as head of the Office, shall have responsibility for the leadership and management of the Office in coordination with the State agency, and, where applicable, any other agency carrying out the Ombudsman program, as follows.

(a) Functions. The Ombudsman shall, personally or through representatives of the Office—

- **(1)** Identify, investigate, and resolve complaints that—
  - **(i)** Are made by, or on behalf of, residents; and
  - **(ii)** Relate to action, inaction, or decisions, that may adversely affect the health, safety, welfare, or rights of residents (including the welfare and rights of residents with respect to the appointment and activities of resident representatives) of—
    - **(A)** Providers, or representatives of providers, of long-term care;
    - **(B)** Public agencies; or
    - **(C)** Health and social service agencies.
- **(2)** Provide services to protect the health, safety, welfare, and rights of the residents;

Functions and Responsibilities: Obtaining Services

- **(3)** Inform residents about means of obtaining services provided by the Ombudsman program;
- **(4)** Ensure that residents have regular and timely access to the services provided through the Ombudsman program and that residents and complainants receive timely responses from representatives of the Office to requests for information and complaints;

Functions and Responsibilities: Address legislative issues

- **(5)** Represent the interests of residents before governmental agencies, assure that individual residents have access to, and pursue (as the Ombudsman determines as necessary and consistent with resident interests) administrative, legal, and other remedies to protect the health, safety, welfare, and rights of residents;
- **(6)** Provide administrative and technical assistance to representatives of the Office and agencies hosting local Ombudsman entities;
- **(7)(i)** Analyze, comment on, and monitor the development and implementation of Federal, State, and local laws, regulations, and other governmental policies and actions, that pertain to the health, safety, welfare, and rights of the residents, with respect to the adequacy of long-term care facilities and services in the State;
  - **(ii)** Recommend any changes in such laws, regulations, policies, and actions as the Office determines to be appropriate; and
  - **(iii)** Facilitate public comment on the laws, regulations, policies, and actions;
  - **(iv)** Provide leadership to statewide systems advocacy efforts of the Office on behalf of long-term care facility residents, including coordination of systems advocacy efforts carried out by representatives of the Office; and
  - **(v)** Provide information to public and private agencies, legislators, the media, and other persons, regarding the problems

and concerns of residents and recommendations related to the problems and concerns.

- o **(vi)** Such determinations and positions shall be those of the Office and shall not necessarily represent the determinations or positions of the State agency or other agency in which the Office is organizationally located.

- o **(vii)** In carrying out systems advocacy efforts of the Office on behalf of long- term care facility residents and pursuant to the receipt of grant funds under the Act, the provision of information, recommendations of changes of laws to legislators, and recommendations of changes of regulations and policies to government agencies by the Ombudsman or representatives of the Office do not constitute lobbying activities as defined by 45 CFR part 93.

- o

Functions and Responsibilities: Promote Citizen Organizations

(8) Coordinate with and promote the development of citizen organizations consistent with the interests of residents; and

Functions and Responsibilities: Support Resident and Family Groups

(9) Promote, provide technical support for the development of, and provide ongoing support as requested by resident and family councils to protect the well-being and rights of residents; and

- • **(b)** The Ombudsman shall be the head of a unified statewide program and shall:
  - o **(1)** Establish or recommend policies, procedures and standards for administration of the Ombudsman program pursuant to § 1327.11(e);

o **(2)** Require representatives of the Office to fulfill the duties set forth in § 1327.19 in accordance with Ombudsman program policies and procedures.

Functions and Responsibilities: Designation of Local Services

- **(c) Designation**. The Ombudsman shall determine designation, and refusal, suspension, or removal of designation, of local Ombudsman entities and representatives of the Office pursuant to section 712(a)(5) of the Act and the policies and procedures set forth in § 1327.11(e)(6).
  - o **(1)** Where an Ombudsman chooses to designate local Ombudsman entities, the Ombudsman shall:
    - **(i)** Designate local Ombudsman entities to be organizationally located within public or nonprofit private entities;
    - **(ii)** Review and approve plans or contracts governing local Ombudsman entity operations, including, where applicable, through area agency on aging plans, in coordination with the State agency; and
    - **(iii)** Monitor, on a regular basis, the Ombudsman program performance of local Ombudsman entities.

Functions and Responsibilities: Training

(2) Training requirements. The Ombudsman shall establish procedures for training for certification and continuing education of the representatives of the Office, based on model standards established by the Director of the Office of Long Term Care Ombudsman Programs as described in section 201(d) of the Act, in consultation with residents, resident representatives, citizen organizations, long term care providers, and the State agency, that—

- **(i)** Specify a minimum number of hours of initial training;

- **(ii)** Specify the content of the training, including training relating to Federal, State, and local laws, regulations, and policies, with respect to long term care facilities in the State; investigative and resolution techniques; and such other matters as the Office determines to be appropriate; and
- **(iii)** Specify an annual number of hours of inservice training for all representatives of the Office;

(3) Prohibit any representative of the Office from carrying out the duties described in § 1327.19 unless the representative—

- **(i)** Has received the training required under paragraph (c)(2) of this section or is performing such duties under supervision of the Ombudsman or a designated representative of the Office as part of certification training requirements; and
- **(ii)** Has been approved by the Ombudsman as qualified to carry out the activity on behalf of the Office;

The Ombudsman Shall Investigate Misconduct by Local Ombudsmen

(4) The Ombudsman shall investigate allegations of misconduct by representatives of the Office in the performance of Ombudsman program duties and, as applicable, coordinate such investigations with the State agency in which the Office is organizationally located, agency hosting the local Ombudsman entity and/or the local Ombudsman entity.

(5) Policies, procedures, or practices which the Ombudsman determines to be in conflict with the laws, policies, or procedures governing the Ombudsman program shall be sufficient grounds for refusal, suspension, or removal of designation of the representative of the Office and/or the local Ombudsman entity.

Annual Report

(g) Annual report. The Ombudsman shall independently develop and provide final approval of an annual report as set forth in section 712(h)(1) of the Act and as otherwise required by the Assistant Secretary.

- **(1)** Such report shall:
  - o **(i)** Describe the activities carried out by the Office in the year for which the report is prepared;
  - o **(ii)** Contain analysis of Ombudsman program data;
  - o **(iii)** Describe evaluation of the problems experienced by, and the complaints made by or on behalf of, residents;
  - o **(iv)** Contain policy, regulatory, and/or legislative recommendations for improving quality of the care and life of the residents; protecting the health, safety, welfare, and rights of the residents; and resolving resident complaints and identified problems or barriers;
  - o **(v)** Contain analysis of the success of the Ombudsman program, including success in providing services to residents of, assisted living, board and care facilities and other similar adult care facilities; and
  - o **(vi)** Describe barriers that prevent the optimal operation of the Ombudsman program.
- **(2)** The Ombudsman shall make such report available to the public and submit it to the Assistant Secretary, the chief executive officer of the State, the State legislature, the State agency responsible for licensing or certifying long term care facilities, and other appropriate governmental entities.

State Responsibilities: State and Local Plans

(a) In addition to the responsibilities set forth in part 1321 of this chapter, the State agency shall ensure that the Ombudsman complies with the relevant provisions of the Act and of this rule.

(b) The State agency shall ensure, through the development of policies, procedures, and other means, consistent with § 1327.11(e)(2), that the Ombudsman program has sufficient authority and access to facilities, residents, and information needed to fully perform all of the functions, responsibilities, and duties of the Office.

(c) The State agency shall provide opportunities for training for the Ombudsman and representatives of the Office in order to maintain expertise to serve as effective advocates for residents. The State agency may utilize funds appropriated under Title III and/ or Title VII of the Act designated for direct services in order to provide access to such training opportunities.

(d) The State agency shall provide personnel supervision and management for the Ombudsman and representatives of the Office who are employees of the State agency. Such management shall include an assessment of whether the Office is performing all of its functions under the Act.

(e) The State agency shall provide monitoring, as required by § 1321.11(b) of this chapter, including but not limited to fiscal monitoring, where the Office and/or local Ombudsman entity is organizationally located within an agency under contract or other arrangement with the State agency. Such monitoring shall include an assessment of whether the Ombudsman program is performing all of the functions, responsibilities and duties set forth in §§ 1327.13 and 1327.19. The State agency may make reasonable requests of reports, including aggregated data regarding Ombudsman program activities, to meet the requirements of this provision.

(f) The State agency shall ensure that any review of files, records or other information maintained by the Ombudsman program is consistent with the disclosure limitations set forth in §§ 1327.11(e)(3) and 1327.13(e).

State Responsibilities: Integration With Other Agencies

(g) The State agency shall integrate the goals and objectives of the Office into the State plan and coordinate the goals and objectives of the Office with those of other programs established under Title VII of the Act and other State elder rights, disability rights, and elder justice programs, including, but not limited to, legal assistance programs provided under section 306(a)(2)(C) of the Act, to promote collaborative efforts and diminish duplicative efforts. Where applicable, the State agency shall require inclusion of goals and objectives of local Ombudsman entities into area plans on aging.

(h) The State agency shall provide elder rights leadership. In so doing, it shall require the coordination of Ombudsman program services with, the activities of other programs authorized by Title VII of the Act as well as other State and local entities with responsibilities relevant to the health, safety, well being or rights of older adults, including residents of long term care facilities as set forth in §1327.13(h).

State Responsibilities: Interference, Retaliation, and Reprisals

(i) The State agency shall:

- **(1)** Ensure that it has mechanisms to prohibit and investigate allegations of interference, retaliation and reprisals:
  - **(i)** by a long term care facility, other entity, or individual with respect to any resident, employee, or other person for filing a complaint with, providing information to, or otherwise cooperating with any representative of the Office; or
  - **(ii)** by a long term care facility, other entity or individual against the Ombudsman or representatives of the Office for fulfillment of the functions, responsibilities, or duties enumerated at §§ 1327.13 and 1327.19; and
- **(2)** Provide for appropriate sanctions with respect to interference, retaliation and reprisals.

State Responsibilities: Legal Counsel

(1) The State agency shall ensure that:

- **(i)** Legal counsel for the Ombudsman program is adequate, available, has competencies relevant to the legal needs of the program and of residents, and is without conflict of interest (as defined by the State ethical standards governing the legal profession), in order to—
  - **(A)** Provide consultation and representation as needed in order for the Ombudsman program to protect the health, safety, welfare, and rights of residents; and
  - **(B)** Provide consultation and/or representation as needed to assist the Ombudsman and representatives of the Office in the performance of their official functions, responsibilities, and duties, including, but not limited to, complaint resolution and systems advocacy;
- **(ii)** The Ombudsman and representatives of the Office assist residents in seeking administrative, legal, and other appropriate remedies. In so doing, the Ombudsman shall coordinate with the legal services developer, legal services providers, and victim assistance services to promote the availability of legal counsel to residents; and
- **(iii)** Legal representation, arranged by or with the approval of the Ombudsman, is provided to the Ombudsman or any representative of the Office against whom suit or other legal action is brought or threatened to be brought in connection with the performance of the official duties.

(2) Such legal counsel may be provided by one or more entities, depending on the nature of the competencies and services needed and as necessary to avoid conflicts of interest (as defined by the State ethical standards governing the legal profession). However, at a minimum, the Office shall have access to an attorney knowledgeable about the Federal and State laws protecting the rights of residents and governing long term care facilities.

(3) Legal representation of the Ombudsman program by the Ombudsman or representative of the Office who is a licensed attorney shall not by itself constitute sufficiently adequate legal counsel.

(4) The communications between the Ombudsman and legal counsel are subject to attorney client privilege.

State Responsibilities: Require Ombudsman to Evaluate and Comment on Laws, Regulations, and Policies

(k) The State agency shall require the Office to:

- **(2)** Analyze, comment on, and monitor the development and implementation of Federal, State, and local laws, regulations, and other government policies and actions that pertain to long term care facilities and services, and to the health, safety, welfare, and rights of residents, in the State, and recommend any changes in such laws, regulations, and policies as the Office determines to be appropriate;
- **(3)** Provide such information as the Office determines to be necessary to public and private agencies, legislators, the media, and other persons, regarding the problems and concerns of individuals residing in long-term care facilities; and recommendations related to such problems and concerns; and

Coordinate Ombudsman Program with other entities

(5) Coordinate Ombudsman program services with entities with responsibilities relevant to the health, safety, welfare, and rights of residents of long-term care facilities, as set forth in § 1327.13(h).

Responsibilities of Agencies Hosting Local Ombudsman Entities

(a) The agency in which a local Ombudsman entity is organizationally located shall be responsible for the personnel management, but not the programmatic oversight, of representatives, including employee and volunteer representatives, of the Office.

(b) The agency in which a local Ombudsman entity is organizationally located shall not have personnel policies or practices which prohibit the representatives of the Office from performing the duties, or from adhering to the access, confidentiality and disclosure requirements of section 712 of the Act, as implemented through this rule and the policies and procedures of the Office.

- **(1)** Policies, procedures and practices, including personnel management practices of the host agency, which the Ombudsman determines conflict with the laws or policies governing the Ombudsman program shall be sufficient grounds for the refusal, suspension, or removal of the designation of local Ombudsman entity by the Ombudsman.
- **(2)** Nothing in this provision shall prohibit the host agency from requiring that the representatives of the Office adhere to the personnel policies and procedures of the agency which are otherwise lawful.

Duties of the Representatives of the Office

In carrying out the duties of the Office, the Ombudsman may designate an entity as a local Ombudsman entity and may designate an employee or volunteer of the local Ombudsman entity as a representative of the Office. Representatives of the Office may also be designated employees or volunteers within the Office.

(a) Duties. An individual so designated as a representative of the Office shall, in accordance with the policies and procedures established by the Office and the State agency:

- **(1)** Identify, investigate, and resolve complaints made by or on behalf of residents that relate to action, inaction, or decisions, that may adversely affect the health, safety, welfare, or rights of the residents;
- **(2)** Provide services to protect the health, safety, welfare, and rights of residents;
- **(3)** Ensure that residents in the service area of the local Ombudsman entity have regular and timely access to the services

provided through the Ombudsman program and that residents and complainants receive timely responses to requests for information and complaints

Represent the Interests of Residents

(4) Represent the interests of residents before government agencies and assure that individual residents have access to, and pursue (as the representative of the Office determines necessary and consistent with resident interest) administrative, legal, and other remedies to protect the health, safety, welfare, and rights of the residents;

(5)(i) Review, and if necessary, comment on any existing and proposed laws, regulations, and other government policies and actions, that pertain to the rights and well being of residents; and

- **(ii)** Facilitate the ability of the public to comment on the laws, regulations, policies, and actions;

Support Resident and Family Councils

(6) Promote, provide technical support for the development of, and provide ongoing support as requested by resident and family councils; and

Complaint Processing

b) (1) With respect to identifying, investigating and resolving complaints, and regardless of the source of the complaint (i.e. complainant), the Ombudsman and the representatives of the Office serve the resident of a long-term care facility. The Ombudsman or representative of the Office shall investigate a complaint, including but not limited to a complaint related to abuse, neglect, or exploitation, for the purposes of resolving the complaint to the resident's satisfaction and of protecting the health, welfare, and rights of the resident. The Ombudsman or representative of the Office may identify, investigate and resolve a complaint impacting multiple residents or all residents of a facility.

(2) Regardless of the source of the complaint (i.e. the complainant), including when the source is the Ombudsman or representative of the Office, the Ombudsman or representative of the Office must support and maximize resident participation in the process of resolving the complaint as follows:

- **(i)** The Ombudsman or representative of Office shall offer privacy to the resident for the purpose of confidentially providing information and hearing, investigating and resolving complaints.
- **(ii)** The Ombudsman or representative of the Office shall personally discuss the complaint with the resident (and, if the resident is unable to communicate informed consent, the resident's representative) in order to:
  - ○ **(A)** Determine the perspective of the resident (or resident representative, where applicable) of the complaint;
  - ○ **(B)** Request the resident (or resident representative, where applicable) to communicate informed consent in order to investigate the complaint;
  - ○ **(C)** Determine the wishes of the resident (or resident representative, where applicable) with respect to resolution of the complaint, including whether the allegations are to be reported and, if so, whether Ombudsman or representative of the Office may disclose resident identifying information or other relevant information to the facility and/or appropriate agencies. Such report and disclosure shall be consistent with paragraph (b)(3) of this section;
  - ○ **(D)** Advise the resident (and resident representative, where applicable) of the resident's rights;
  - ○ **(E)** Work with the resident (or resident representative, where applicable) to develop a plan of action for resolution of the complaint;
  - ○ **(F)** Investigate the complaint to determine whether the complaint can be verified; and
  - ○ **(G)** Determine whether the complaint is resolved to the satisfaction of the resident (or resident representative, where applicable).

- **(iii)**Where the resident is unable to communicate informed consent, and has no resident representative, the Ombudsman or representative of the Office shall:
  - o **(A)** Take appropriate steps to investigate and work to resolve the complaint in order to protect the health, safety, welfare and rights of the resident; and
  - o **(B)** Determine whether the complaint was resolved to the satisfaction of the complainant.
- **(iv)** In determining whether to rely upon a resident representative to communicate or make determinations on behalf of the resident related to complaint processing, the Ombudsman or representative of the Office shall ascertain the extent of the authority that has been granted to the resident representative under court order (in the case of a guardian or conservator), by power of attorney or other document by which the resident has granted authority to the representative, or under other applicable State or Federal law.

(3) The Ombudsman or representative of the Office may provide information regarding the complaint to another agency in order for such agency to substantiate the facts for regulatory, protective services, law enforcement, or other purposes so long as the Ombudsman or representative of the Office adheres to the disclosure requirements of section 712(d) of the Act and the procedures set forth in § 1327.11(e)(3).

Assisting Contact With Another Entity

- **(i)** Where the goals of a resident or resident representative are for regulatory, protective services or law enforcement action, and the Ombudsman or representative of the Office determines that the resident or resident representative has communicated informed consent to the Office, the Office must assist the resident or resident representative in contacting the appropriate agency and/ or disclose the information for which the resident has provided consent to the appropriate agency for such purposes.
- **(ii)** Where the goals of a resident or resident representative can be served by disclosing information to a facility representative and/or

referrals to an entity other than those referenced in paragraph (b)(3)(i) of this section, and the Ombudsman or representative of the Office determines that the resident or resident representative has communicated informed consent to the Ombudsman program, the Ombudsman or representative of the Office may assist the resident or resident representative in contacting the appropriate facility representative or the entity, provide information on how a resident or representative may obtain contact information of such facility representatives or entities, and/or disclose the information for which the resident has provided consent to an appropriate facility representative or entity, consistent with Ombudsman program procedures.

Ombudsmen Are Not Mandatory Reporters of Abuse

- **(iii)** In order to comply with the wishes of the resident, (or, in the case where the resident is unable to communicate informed consent, the wishes of the resident representative), the Ombudsman and representatives of the Office shall not report suspected abuse, neglect or exploitation of a resident when a resident or resident representative has not communicated informed consent to such report except as set forth in paragraphs (b)(5) through (7) of this section, notwithstanding State laws to the contrary.

Informed Consent

(4) For purposes of paragraphs (b)(1) through (3) of this section, communication of informed consent may be made in writing, including through the use of auxiliary aids and services. Alternatively, communication may be made orally or visually, including through the use of auxiliary aids and services, and such consent must be documented contemporaneously by the Ombudsman or a representative of the Office, in accordance with the procedures of the Office

(5) For purposes of paragraphs (b)(1) paragraph (3) of this section, if a resident is unable to communicate his or her informed consent, or perspective on the extent to which the matter has been satisfactorily resolved, the Ombudsman or representative of the Office may rely on the communication of informed consent and/or perspective regarding the resolution of the complaint of a resident representative so long as the Ombudsman or representative of the Office has no reasonable cause to believe that the resident representative is not acting in the best interests of the resident.

(6) For purposes of paragraphs (b)(1)

through (3) of this section, the procedures for disclosure, as required by § 1327.11(e)(3), shall provide that the Ombudsman or representative of the Office may refer the matter and disclose resident identifying information to the appropriate agency or agencies for regulatory oversight; protective services; access to administrative, legal, or other remedies; and/or law enforcement action in the following circumstances:

- **(i)** The resident is unable to communicate informed consent to the Ombudsman or representative of the Office;
- **(ii)** The resident has no resident representative;
- **(iii)** The Ombudsman or representative of the Office has reasonable cause to believe that an action, inaction or decision may adversely affect the health, safety, welfare, or rights of the resident;
- **(iv)** The Ombudsman or representative of the Office has no evidence indicating that the resident would not wish a referral to be made;
- **(v)** The Ombudsman or representative of the Office has reasonable cause to believe that it is in the best interest of the resident to make a referral; and
- **(vi)** The representative of the Office obtains the approval of the Ombudsman or otherwise follows the policies and procedures of the Office described in paragraph (b)(9) of this section.

(7) For purposes of paragraphs (b)(1) through (3) of this section, the procedures for disclosure, as required by § 1327.11(e)(3), shall provide that, the Ombudsman or representative of the Office may refer the matter and disclose resident identifying information to the appropriate agency or agencies for regulatory oversight; protective services; access to administrative, legal, or other remedies; and/or law enforcement action in the following circumstances:

- **(i)** The resident is unable to communicate informed consent to the Ombudsman or representative of the Office and has no resident representative, or the Ombudsman or representative of the Office has reasonable cause to believe that the resident representative has taken an action, inaction or decision that may adversely affect the health, safety, welfare, or rights of the resident;
- **(ii)** The Ombudsman or representative of the Office has no evidence indicating that the resident would not wish a referral to be made;
- **(iii)** The Ombudsman or representative of the Office has reasonable cause to believe that it is in the best interest of the resident to make a referral; and
- **(iv)** The representative of the Ombudsman obtains the approval of the Ombudsman.

(8) The procedures for disclosure, as required by § 1327.11(e)(3), shall provide that, if the Ombudsman or representative of the Office personally witnesses suspected abuse, gross neglect, or exploitation of a resident, the Ombudsman or representative of the Office shall seek communication of informed consent from such resident to disclose resident identifying information to appropriate agencies;

- **(i)** Where such resident is able to communicate informed consent, or has a resident representative available to provide informed consent, the Ombudsman or representative of the Office shall follow the direction of the resident or resident representative as set forth paragraphs (b)(1) through (3) of this section; and
- **(ii)** Where the resident is unable to communicate informed consent, and has no resident representative available to provide informed consent, the Ombudsman or representative of the Office shall open a case with the Ombudsman or representative of the Office as the complainant, follow the Ombudsman program's complaint resolution procedures, and shall refer the matter and disclose identifying information of the resident to the management of the facility in which the resident resides and/or to the appropriate

agency or agencies for substantiation of abuse, gross neglect or exploitation in the following circumstances:

- o **(A)** The Ombudsman or representative of the Office has no evidence indicating that the resident would not wish a referral to be made;
- o **(B)** The Ombudsman or representative of the Office has reasonable cause to believe that disclosure would be in the best interest of the resident; and
- o **(C)** The representative of the Office obtains the approval of the Ombudsman or otherwise follows the policies and procedures of the Office described in paragraph (b)(9) of this section.
- **(iii)** In addition, the Ombudsman or representative of the Office, following the policies and procedures of the Office described in paragraph (b)(9) of this section, may report the suspected abuse, gross neglect, or exploitation to other appropriate agencies for regulatory oversight; protective services; access to administrative, legal, or other remedies; and/or law enforcement action.

(9) Prior to disclosing resident identifying information pursuant to paragraph (b)(6) or (8) of this section, a representative of the Office must obtain approval by the Ombudsman or, alternatively, follow policies and procedures of the Office which provide for such disclosure.

- **(i)** Where the policies and procedures require Ombudsman approval, they shall include a time frame in which the Ombudsman is required to communicate approval or disapproval in order to assure that the representative of the Office has the ability to promptly take actions to protect the health, safety, welfare or rights of residents. . .

Conflicts of Interest—OMITTED

There is considerable information in this section. Use the URL at the end of this section to see the entire regulation.

Helpful URLs

You may need to copy a URL and paste it into your browser window.

Surveyors Guidelines: Center for Medicare and Medicaid Services: State Operations Handbook, Appendix PP–Guidance to Surveyors for Long Term Care Facilities (Used in this handbook)   Since these guidelines are updated fairly regularly on about a 6 month basis, it is wise to check periodically for additional information. These updates affect only the guidance materials and do not affect the actual regulations unless changes to those regulations have been publicly announced.

https://www.cms.gov/Medicare/Provider-Enrollment-and-Certification/GuidanceforLawsAndRegulations/Downloads/Advance-Appendix-PP-Including-Phase-2-.pdf

CMS Regional Offices

http://www.cms.gov/About-CMS/Agency-Information/RegionalOffices/index.html?redirect=/regionaloffices/

State Operations Manual Chapter 7 - Survey and Enforcement Process for Skilled Nursing Facilities and Nursing Facilities

http://www.cms.gov/Regulations-and-Guidance/Guidance/Manuals/downloads/som107c07.pdf

Electronic Code of Federal Nursing Home Regulations: Title 42; Chapter IV; Subchapter G; Part 483–Requirements for states and long term care facilities

http://www.ecfr.gov/cgi-bin/text-idx?tpl=/ecfrbrowse/Title42/42cfr483_main_02.tpl

Federal Regulations for the Long-Term Care Ombudsman Programs.   45 CRF Parts 1321 and 1327

https://www.federalregister.gov/documents/2015/02/11/2015-01914/state-long-term-care-ombudsman-programs

COMAR: Code of Maryland: (suggest using the "Access through Table of contents Structure)

http://www.dsd.state.md.us/COMAR/ComarHome.html

LexisNexis: Unannotated Code of Maryland and Rules (These are the laws of Maryland. You would mostly use the Health General section. Click in the open box next to Health General, then click on the + to open that section. Click on Title 19. Health Care Facilities. Click then on the section you need, nursing homes, assisted living facilities, etc.)

This same URL will take you to the laws governing the operations of the State Ombudsman Program in the Human Services section

http://www.lexisnexis.com/hottopics/mdcode/

Regulations in Washington DC

https://doh.dc.gov/publication/nursing-homes-regulations